Moving

Toward

Stillness

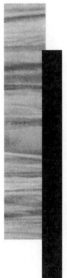

Moving Toward Stillness

Lessons in Daily Life from the Martial Ways of Japan

Dave Lowry

TUTTLE PUBLISHING
Tokyo • Rutland, Vermont • Singapore

First published in 2000 by Tuttle Publishing, an imprint of Periplus Editions (HK) Ltd., with editorial offices at 364 Innovation Drive, North Clarendon, Vermont 05759.

Library of Congress Cataloging-in-Publication Data

Lowry, Dave.
   Moving toward stillness : lessons in daily life from the martial ways of Japan / Dave Lowry—Ist. ed.
    185 p. ; 23 cm.
   I. Martial arts—Japan—Philosophy. 2. Bushido. I. Title.
GVII00.77.A2L66 2000
796.8/0952 21   99-29183
                            CIP

ISBN-10: 0-8048-3160-2
ISBN-13: 978-0-8048-3160-4

Distributed by:

North America, Latin America & Europe
Tuttle Publishing
364 Innovation Drive
North Clarendon, VT 05759-9436
Tel: (802) 773-8930
Fax: (802) 773-6993
info@tuttlepublishing.com
www.tuttlepublishing.com

Japan
Tuttle Publishing
Yaekari Building, 3rd Floor
5-4-12 Ōsaki
Shinagawa-ku
Tokyo 141 0032
Tel: (03) 5437-0171
Fax: (03) 5437-0755
tuttle-sales@gol.com

Asia Pacific
Berkeley Books Pte. Ltd.
130 Joo Seng Road
#06-01/03 Olivine Building
Singapore 368357
Tel: (65) 6280-1330
Fax: (65) 6280-6290
inquiries@periplus.com.sg
www.periplus.com

Indonesia
PT Java Books Indonesia
Kawasan Industri Pulogadung
JI. Rawa Gelam IV No. 9
Jakarta 13930, Indonesia
Tel: (62-21) 4682-1088
Fax: (62-21) 461-0207
cs@javabooks.co.id

09 08 07 06   10 9 8 7 6
Design by Mary Burgess
Printed in the United States of America

TUTTLE PUBLISHING ® is a registered trademark of Tuttle Publishing, a division of Periplus Editions (HK) Ltd.

CONTENTS

Stand ye in the ways,

and see, and ask for

the old paths, where

is the good way,

and walk therein.

— Jeremiah 6:16

Introduction

In 1986 *Black Belt* magazine's editor, Jim Coleman, asked me to write a monthly column for the magazine. Although he told me that the title of the column was to be "The Karate Way," he gave me a wide rein; I needn't confine myself to the art of karate-do. I was free to cover the whole range of the experience of the Japanese martial Ways, the *budo*. I did, and more than ten years later I am still at it. He is surprised by this, I think, and in a way, so am I. But as I have continued to travel the path they provide, the budo have been a source of inspiration in so many areas of my life that it seems there is always something to write about concerning them, always more roads to explore along the journey, more of their vistas to experience and appreciate. I am convinced that I will continue to discover new ideas and to come to look at old ones in fresh ways so long as I continue my practice of the budo.

Putting together some of the columns I have written over the past decade as I have here, I was struck by the fact that a lot of my writing has a, oh, I don't know. . . *curmudgeonly* tone to it. I often found myself in these essays excoriating the West and describing with a certain disdain many of the "non-Japanese" attitudes toward the martial Ways I have seen. I see it myself in my words, so I would perforce plead guilty to these transgressions. But I am by no means anti-American, nor do I believe that the involvement of non-Japanese practitioners in the Japanese budo has been an entirely or even a predominantly negative force in these Ways. I do believe this: I think the martial paths that have been paved by the founders of these extraordinary disciplines have an immeasurable value for modern men and women no matter where they are from. The value of these Ways in no small part springs from the social mores they seek to refine in those who follow them. To pursue these Ways without a cognizance of all they offer, not just in terms of the physical realm but in the spiritual and psychological dimensions as well, is a waste of time and a regrettable misuse of the budo.

What I rail against is not Westernism or Westerners involved in these Ways. My quarrel is with modernism, a spirit that demands instant results, that values the ego of the individual over all else, that runs roughshod over long and painstakingly established methods and goals without taking the time to investigate or to appreciate those methods and goals. Modernism is in no way confined to Western culture; the Japanese of today are very often equally thoughtless, boorish, crass. For those of you who would follow a martial Way, no matter what your background, I have advocated in this essay that you study the budo in the spirit of those who laid the path in the first place. Try to understand the Ways as your predecessors did, as much as possible, and try to apply the lessons of the journey to the many other areas of your life.

If we are serious about the martial Ways of Japan, they cannot be activities for which we schedule a couple of nights a week, entertainments or diversions or the combative equivalent of a get-in-shape program. They offer a way of living, one with ramifications in every area of life, every moment of it, that can hold tremendous rewards. In the essays collected in this book I present some of the lessons the budo have to teach us day by day.

So forgive me my cranky tone in the essays that follow, please. I hope they will be of interest and of some use for the reader. And in the next ten years of my writing—if I make it that long—I promise I will make an effort to be a bit more sunny.

Chapter One

Entering the Doorway

"A man is judged by how he opens a door,
and a woman is judged by how she shuts it."

To understand the meaning behind this curious saying we must know
something about doors and the architecture of premodern Japan. Unlike the
hinged doors of Western-style buildings, Japanese doors slide back and forth
along grooved wooden tracks in the floor. In some rooms, the door might be
a small rectangle, providing an opening so tiny that one must virtually crawl
through it on one's hands and knees. These little doors are called *nijiri guchi*;
they are a common feature in the traditional tea house used for the ritual of
making and drinking tea, or *chado*. Part of the tea ceremony involves making a humble entrance to the house itself. Scooting through the small opening on one's hands and knees serves as a way of humbling oneself and deflat-
ing the ego. (Considering the size of some of the egos passing into them
today, if we could install nijiri guchi in the doorways of the *dojo*, or martial
arts training halls, to be found in this country, it would doubtless be the
most wonderful architectural improvement imaginable for those structures.)
Traditional Japanese buildings also have doors that span entire walls or are
room partitions that can be slid back to double the size of a room. No matter what their size or shape, Japanese doors of all kinds are opened in the
same way: you kneel at the crack of the door and push it open, then you

come into the room by sliding forward on your knees.

This is quite a simplified description of entering a room, as any exponent of a truly classical Way or art of Japan will tell you. *Sukisha*—well-bred people—know that you must use the hand nearest the door to open it a few inches ("the length of a forefinger," to be exact, according to one feudal school of etiquette), then you switch hands to slide it back the rest of the way. There are all kinds of manners to be observed in this simple action of opening a door and coming into a room if you are to observe the protocol of ancient Japan. The point is, to the Japanese of the feudal period, even an ordinary, everyday task like entering a room had a significance and a prescribed order that evolved about it. It is no exaggeration to say that when performed with the proper spirit and mental attitude this mundane action could assume the proportions of a *kata*, one of the formal movements that are the foundation for all the Japanese arts and Ways. And the meaning of the expression that a man is judged by how he opens a door and a woman by how she shuts it is found in that spirit and attitude.

Look at it this way: it would be very easy to make a flashy, imposing entrance through a Japanese style door. You could sling open the door along its track with a vigorous shove, banging it against the supporting frame with a dramatic *thump!* Remember, too, that people sit on the floor in a traditional Japanese home. If you come striding into the room standing up, you are going to tower over everyone sitting there. You will be imposing. You will have the attention of everyone in the room. Literally, everyone there would, indeed, be in the position of looking up to you. To many, this would, indeed, seem a most attractive way to "make an entrance," so they must wonder why it is that Japanese etiquette demands just the opposite.

The answer is that manners in Japan, a good many of them at least, have always been directed at maintaining and preserving social harmony. Getting along with the other fellow was important, and important, too, was the concept that the individual self was not so significant as the welfare of the group. (Of course, these motivations have guided the etiquette of most civilizations. In Japan, however, they were paramount. Rice, always the staple grain of the

Japanese diet, is so labor-intensive to cultivate that communal work and living was a necessity. This led to patterns of settlement where people spent much of their lives close by others. In many ways, the etiquette of traditional Japan served as a lubricant against the inevitable social frictions of daily life.) The higher in the social order the individual, then, the more humble and self-effacing he often was in his conduct. The "classier" the person, the less he needed to display himself.

The individual who was secure in his social caste did not need to remind himself or others of his position constantly. When he came into a room, it was not necessary to use the entrance as an occasion for drawing attention to himself. He came in quietly, using first one hand and then the other to open the door, because that method allowed the door to be moved softly, with minimal noise. He entered using a sliding shuffle on his knees because that kept him at a level equal to others already in the room.

This is the meaning behind the saying that a man could be judged by how he entered a room. But why the distinction between men and women? Does the adage imply there was a different standard of manners between the sexes? Well, yes, to some degree. Women were often in subordinate positions in daily life in old Japan. If a group of men were in a room, it would likely be a woman who served food and drink and who would then leave. So a woman would be leaving a room more often, closing the door behind her while there were still people inside. Hence the distinction between the sexes in the expression. But that distinction can be misleading. In essence, gender is superfluous. What matters is the spirit and attitude with which one conducts him-or herself.

This spirit and attitude has pervaded Japanese culture, and since the budo are a product of that culture, it should hardly be surprising that such concepts are an integral part of the martial Ways as well. And doubtless that is why it is so disappointing and saddening to see so many people who presumably are serious about making the budo a meaningful part of their lives yet who so determinedly remain ignorant of this spirit and attitude or who, worse still, deliberately choose to disregard it. Whenever you see a martial arts "master" come strutting onto the dojo floor as if the world were fortunate to have him in it, or a competitor at a budo competition come prancing out of the square with his hands held triumphantly aloft, you are witness to such ignorance, such arrogant disregard for the traditions in which the budo were developed.

The skills of opening and closing a sliding Japanese door are a part of *reishiki*, "proper form," or "etiquette." The ability to move in a balanced and graceful way by sliding one's knees on the floor is a specific aspect of this form, this mastery of the self that allows us to get along with others and to present ourselves to the world in a respectful way. To the regret of those of us who have an interest in, a feel for the traditions of old Japan, these are skills and abilities that have largely disappeared in the modern world. Those who are still conversant with these traditions tend to be exponents of the classical arts, like the budo and tea ceremony, people willing to spend the time to learn methods that are in actual practice of limited value. Unless you are living in Japan, and even there nowadays, knowing how to open a sliding door and how to go in and out of it are not, to be sure, vital in day-to-day affairs. But still some manners, what D'Avenant called those "unwritten laws by which the people keep even kings in awe," have a way of transcending time and immediate circumstance. In any era, any culture, we are all judged by the little things we do. Things like entering and leaving a building. We who set out to follow the path set by the Japanese martial Ways are especially conscious of this, knowing that outer form is so often an expression of a deeper inner state. This should give you something to think about when you enter a room or close a door, whether you turn the knob or push the handle or slide the door along a track.

Chapter Two

The Way of the Master

Yes, yes, I know. This is supposed to be about martial arts, and no one has ever accused me of being a competent music critic. Nonetheless, if you have never heard the music of the Japanese musician Kitaro, I would urge you to give it a listen. Kitaro's medium is that of our century's most typically technological of instruments, the synthesizer, backed by all kinds of electronically amplified guitars, violins, and so on. The music itself is of the sort that has been labeled "New Age," lots of lush instrumental passages that soar and crash and sparkle and fade away. It is music that calls to mind images of waves and surf, of winds whistling through forests and across great plains, and probably because of this resonance with the sounds of nature Kitaro's work is becoming popular all over the world.

A few years ago, Kitaro, a native of Japan, made his first concert tour of the United States. The Public Broadcasting System here produced a documentary on the event. It was interesting for Kitaro fans, but I hope that some of my fellow budoka saw it, too. Behind the scenes of Kitaro's life and performances are fascinating glimpses of a master, and whether the path is along the Way of music or the martial Way, the methods of a master are remarkably similar. "Fighting against others is easy; fighting against yourself is hard" and "All of my art is inspired by my desire for harmony with the universe" were comments Kitaro made about his music, but he might just as well have been talking about karate-do or any of the other Japanese budo. Interesting, too, were this Japanese master's interactions with his American accompanists, for the struggles and triumphs they shared are exactly those experienced by Western budoka who train under traditional Japanese instruction.

Kitaro's music seems, like jazz, to be spontaneous and unaffectedly natural. "Everything you do flows from nature," he says, and it is this spontaneity martial artists seek as well. But achieving that effect involves a process that is anything but "natural." "Usually when I work with bands there are absolutely no boundaries on what I can play," says one musician in the documentary who has been hired to accompany Kitaro on the U.S. tour. Not a chance of that happening, responded Kitaro. Like the budo master, Kitaro knew precisely what it was he wanted to create. He was no more interested in the improvised "jamming" offered by the musicians than the karate sensei is interested in the beginner's "insights" into a front kick. The student has nothing to offer but an absolute willingness to do his sensei's bidding, following the teacher's instructions and direction without question or comments or personal improvisation.

American backup musicians for Kitaro were also frustrated when their practice sessions were finished for the day and their leader still remained distant and cool toward them. Said one: "When the job is done, it's done," and he complained of the aloofness he perceived in Kitaro's behavior. "He's just one of us," the musician insisted, sounding exactly like some American budoka talking about their teachers. While class is in session these students have no problem recognizing their sensei as a leader, someone special and different from others. Once out of the dojo, however, they expect to be able to treat him as one of the guys. They are products of a political democracy and are unfamiliar with anything but social and cultural democracies. Nations like Japan, though, do not share this tradition, and Japanese arts and culture do not reflect it at all.

"Does this guy want me to bow down to him every morning?" another musician bitterly complained of Kitaro. The Americans clearly thought this foreign visitor was "uppity." But the student/teacher relationship can never be equal, not according to the traditions of Confucianism on which such relationships are based. And the role of the master is not a forty hour a week job with time off and other benefits to be negotiated. The Way of the master is a Way of life itself. Contrary to the Western notion of the "master" who teaches a class and then goes out with the guys to tie one on and flirt with women, in Japan the master is considered to be a true master only when he is a *shihan*, a "model" for the guys. And so by the very nature of his mastery, while he may socialize and be informal with students, he must always keep a certain distance between himself and his followers.

In the early part of the documentary on Kitaro's American tour the musicians' frustration and anger over these cultural differences is quite obvious. "I'm not a boy," snapped one member of the band in response to Kitaro's criticism. Others protested Kitaro's lack of sensitivity to American ways (ways that they naturally and without examination assumed were in every regard superior). But as time went on and particularly after the tour went to Japan for some performances, the musicians began to see the situation more deeply and broadly. Their perception of Kitaro changed. "He speaks of mountains and rivers, natural things instead of electronic things that we're all used to," one band member commented, summing up perfectly the crucial distinction between a master, who tends to see into the heart of things, and the rest of us, who tend to fuss and fritter with petty gadgets and other mediocre accoutrements. Said the band member of Kitaro, "He lives by the natural part of the universe."

Another member of the backup band confided, "I've probably rehearsed this music for 200 hours. Same music, over and over. I finally realized what [Kitaro is] after: simplicity. And the simpler the music is, the more difficult it is to do." Change the word "music" for "martial art technique" or "kata" and you will see what kind of insights are to be gained in the presence of a master.

And, finally, I heard one of Kitaro's musicians express a thought that (at long last) some senior budoka are beginning to express as well. "I think it is important," one of them said, "for us to have a peripheral view of Japanese culture, for the things it can do for our own culture." This is precisely what I try to do each time I sit down to write about the Japanese martial Ways. And I suppose my comparative lack of success is an obvious sign that I, unlike Kitaro who was able to communicate it so well, am a very long way from mastery.

Chapter Three

The Warrior's Art

I've never seen a Bruce Lee movie.

I realize this may shock a number of readers who revere the late actor. But when his movies were showing in theaters I was a student in school and a *deshi,* a martial arts student. When I wasn't in school or training with my sensei, he always found plenty of chores for me to do, and there just wasn't much time for things like going to the movies. I still have not seen an entire Bruce Lee film, as I said, but I did catch about five minutes' worth of one the other night on the television. And while it would be unfair to make any judgments about it based on those few moments, I have to say that I did find them to be very interesting.

I don't know the name of the movie. But Mr. Lee and a woman companion were in Rome, sightseeing. The woman pointed out the Colosseum and began telling Lee about it. Mr. Lee, however, pointedly turned his back and gazed disinterestedly off into the distance. Later they walked through Rome's garden district where once again Mr. Lee's companion tried to explain the historical and artistic significance of the sights before them. Lee sneered. He called the gardens a waste of space and land. If he owned it, he said, he'd build housing there and make money on the property.

The attitude displayed by Mr. Lee's character said a lot, I think. The message was clear: Martial artists do not have time for sissy stuff like beauty and culture. Art and aesthetics have no value to the warrior.

When I watched that snippet of the film I was reminded of another great old city like Rome, of another architectural wonder like the Colosseum, and of another martial artist. The city I thought of was Nara, Japan's ancient capital. The architecture was the Nandaimon, the Great South Gate of the Todai-ji, the Todai Temple. The gate is a masterpiece, two stories high and supported by eighteen enormous columns. Nandaimon is constructed faithfully according to the principles of the Tenjikuyo style of architecture, which originated in India and was eventually brought to Japan when Buddhist temples were first erected there. (Perhaps you have seen the two guardian Nio statues in karate history books, both of them scowling in martial poses; these figures are ensconced in facing alcoves at the Nandaimon gate.) The warrior I thought of was Minamoto Yoritomo, who was in Nara late in the twelfth century when the huge gate was built. But unlike the martial artist portrayed by Bruce Lee in the movie, Yoritomo undoubtedly would not have sneered and turned his back on the Nandaimon. He was the warrior who was responsible for erecting it.

For the Japanese martial artist of old, the *bugeisha,* and for the more serious of those modern budoka who follow in a similar spirit, art and beauty were not superfluous stuff by any means. The warrior lived in precarious times in Japan. During Japan's civil war, which lasted over two centuries, violent and sudden death could come at any moment. Faced with a constant reminder of their mortality, the bugeisha naturally sought to balance the violence inherent in his life with a keen appreciation for the beauty of the world around him. Like the condemned man who savors his last meal with a special and intense kind of pleasure, the bugeisha relished the opportunities he had to create or to appreciate art. His particular tastes, preferences for the simple, the austere, and the subtle, have had a dramatic and lasting influence on many aspects of Japanese culture that we can still see today. The

Noh theater, garden architecture, clothing design—all of these facets of modern Japanese culture continue to reflect the sensitivities and sensibilities of the warrior.

There are numerous famous examples of the bugeisha's artistic spirit. The great swordsman Miyamoto Musashi, for instance, has left no real legacy in terms of the unique style of swordsmanship he created, but he did leave behind a number of examples of his marvelous calligraphy, his paintings, and his sculpture. Looking at them we understand that just as fierce as Musahi's fighting skills was his drive to create, to make something of value and beauty. Yagyu Renyasai, a headmaster of the Shinkage ryu, that was dominated by his family for generations, was one of the most proficient sword masters of his age, yet he is renowned centuries later for his magnificently forged sword guards with their intricate designs and classic motifs. Uyesugi Kenshin was a ferocious man to face in combat, one of Japan's most brilliant military leaders, but his poetry is still admired for the depth of its quiet passion and profound insights into human nature. One poem he composed at bivouac just before an important battle goes, in part:

Night comes.
Wild geese fly in formation in the moonlight.
The mountains of Etchu are silhouetted against the dreamlike
waves of Noto Bay.

The traditional warrior considered fine arts to be a complement to martial arts. He integrated them into his daily life. He sought to excel in the arts of painting, calligraphy, or the tea ceremony, or at appreciating them. The bugeisha was, by definition, a *sukisha* as well, an "individual of refined and discriminating taste." Of course, there were also brutes among the samurai. There are brutish men in every era, and to be faced with savagery and the threat of dying, to be a professional man-at-arms, will inevitably expose the crude and self-centered nature of some men. Still there is no denying the artistic legacy left by the warrior class of Japan. The samurai, as a whole, did not consider the pursuit of beauty and culture to be a waste of his time, nor did he believe that such activities detracted from the quality of his warrior-ship. The samurai of Japan would not have turned his back on Rome if he had been given the chance to see it. More likely, he would have studied the art and architecture there and learned from it. In the face of beauty, of fine and great things, the real warrior would never have sneered.

Chapter Four

Get a New Wife

I was sitting with a karate sensei in his dojo one afternoon, visiting with him, when he was approached by a fellow who had come to watch the class that day. The fellow said he was interested in taking up karate, but he wondered if training might present a problem for him. He was a marathon runner, he explained, and he spent several hours a week running and traveling to races. Would karate practice interfere with that?

Another time, an acquaintance commented to me that he wanted to begin studying the art of aikido. But as an underpaid schoolteacher, he wasn't sure he could afford the club dues of $30 a month that were levied by the dojo he wanted to join. It is pertinent to add in this case that this acquaintance was a smoker who easily spent more than $30 a month on his habit.

When I encounter these kinds of people, I am always reminded of a falconer I once heard about. Falconry, of course, is the art of raising and training birds of prey—hawks, falcons, and even eagles—to hunt. It is a very, very old art, one that requires a tremendous amount of study into the life and behaviors of these birds. It also demands an amazing patience to tame them and to accommodate their highly strung natures. Falconers typically spend several hours a day with their birds. This falconer met a man who said he wanted to take up falconry but he was afraid that his wife would not adapt well to having a fierce-looking raptor as a permanent addition to their back-yard. What should he do? The falconer's reply: "Get a new wife."

It is, I suppose, indicative of our modern civilization that, if I may para-phrase Churchill, so many wish to have so much while expending so little. We have parents who want to raise perfect children while simultaneously pursuing careers that prevent them from even seeing their offspring for more than a few minutes a day. We have single people who want to establish meaningful, lifelong relationships and who think they can do that by plac-ing a few ostensibly witty lines in a personal ad in a newspaper. And more to the point, we have would-be budoka who expect to reap the benefits of the martial Ways without any real sacrifice. They are, all of them, going to be disappointed.

The truth is, raising good children demands enormous commitment and sacrifices. Healthy, loving relationships cannot be founded on the basis of snappy advertisements. They take time and a willingness to compromise and grow. To make the budo a Way of life requires precisely the same. Those prospective entrants to the Way who think they can make any kind of head-way along its path without sacrifices are fooling themselves.

The falconer's advice on getting a new wife sounds harsh. It was not, I think we can assume, entirely serious. But his point was that an involved and difficult discipline like falconry requires some pretty uncommon dedication. The fellow who asked him the question about taking it up might not actu-ally have had to give up his wife if he wanted to be a falconer. But if he wished to involve himself in that kind of art, he would have to be prepared to make some significant changes in his life. This is because, contrary to pop-ular and frequently voiced opinions, not all the avocations that are available to us are alike. It has been convenient for many martial arts teachers and other such promoters to present the budo as a sort of pastime, a hobby that can be approached exactly as we would bowling or bridge. One can, these types suggest, go down to the neighborhood dojo a couple of nights a week for a quick "workout" and then leave it behind when one walks out the door.

In this regard, martial arts training is envisioned as being similar to joining the types of health clubs or fitness centers we see advertised everywhere. The budo, however, are not like weight lifting and aerobics classes. The goals pursued in the dojo are markedly different from those of the local health or fitness center.

The budo—very difficult to describe in their entirety since we have nothing analogous to them in the West—are a multifaceted discipline. They encompass a rigorous, extremely demanding physical effort, a concerted dedication to old and quite often foreign cultural values, and a willingness to submit to a method of teaching and transmission of knowledge that are wholly unlike the ways to which we are accustomed. Just learning to move across the floor on one's knees, a standard training exercise in aikido, for example, takes years to do correctly and without a lot of discomfort. Concepts of the budo at its higher levels require a serious expenditure of time and energy. No one with less than a decade of constant training and thinking could hope to understand even the basics of some of these concepts. Then, too, because the budo are not native to our country, those qualified to teach them at their upper levels are few and far between. Travel to different cities or to Japan is a must for most budoka at some stage of their training.

All of these factors must be considered by the budoka. None of them are the kind of considerations that are weighed in making an informed decision to take up softball or weight lifting, or any of the more conventional avocations in which those around us may choose to become involved. The budo are not an ordinary pastime. Those who follow them cannot be ordinary, either. So to that marathoner who worried that karate might interfere with his running, I would say, yes, it will. It is the nature of a budo, like karate or any of the rest of them. And if you cannot give the martial arts the time and attention they deserve, the time and attention necessary to make them a meaningful part of your life, then both the budo and you will be better off if you leave them alone. To the fellow who spent money on his smoking habit without complaint but who was hesitant to make an equal investment in aikido training, I cannot imagine, frankly, what to say. Someone with that sense of priorities is likely, I'm afraid, to find that the cost of the budo life is far too high for him to pay, no matter what its price.

Chapter Five

Kantoku ("To Perceive Virtue")

Both my sensei and his wife were practitioners of *chado,* the Way of tea. They taught me the basics of chado, but although they were skilled at it, they were not actually teachers of a formal tradition of the art. So I cannot call myself a *chajin,* a "tea person." Even so, as a student I took an interest in this Way, one so closely affiliated with the budo I had chosen to follow, and I did my best to learn what they tried to teach me about it. One day, however, when Sensei was showing me some variations of the *temae* (the movements of chado, their kata, in other words), I was skeptical. He was explaining specifically *kinin kiyotsugu usucha,* the proper temae for serving tea to a person of nobility or an aristocrat.

"Come on, Sensei," I said. "Do you really think I'm ever going to have a chance to use this? Do you think there's much possibility of me serving tea to a shogun or some daimyo?" It was an impertinent question, of the sort I often asked and my sensei graciously tolerated, but it was a fair one. Feudalism in Japan went out well over a century ago. There wasn't any nobility at my sensei's home. Learning the formal movements of tea preparation and serving for nonexistent people did seem more than a bit anachronistic to me.

"Maybe not," Sensei admitted. "But you will have the chance to use the sense of *kantoku* that serving tea like this can teach you. You can use that many times in your life."

"Kantoku" is an old-fashioned word in Japanese, extremely so. I looked for it in about half a dozen modern Japanese dictionaries recently and found it listed in none of them. It means, literally, "to perceive virtue." The word "Kantoku," if you hear of it at all, is likely to be used in a budo dojo or in another of the Do forms such as flower arranging or the tea ceremony. When used in this context, it refers to a specific quality that has no single word equivalent in English, as far as I know. Grace, composure, awareness, and controlled, powerful vigor: all are components of kantoku.

Kantoku as a concept has its martial origins in *kyujutsu,* the feudal era art of battlefield bowmanship. The seventeenth-century founder of the Yamato ryu of kyujutsu, Morikawa Kozan, wrote that the archer had two goals to pursue. One was excellence in combative skills with the bow, clearly. The second was in the development and perfection of kantoku. Today, of course, the modern martial Way of the bow, or *kyudo* as it is called, is largely a matter of mastering etiquette, mental poise, and various kata that are centered on the shooting of arrows successfully into a fixed target. In the old days of the samurai, though, the warrior always had foremost in his mind the task of delivering his arrows with deadly accuracy to a live enemy who was, he needed to assume, trying to do much the same to him. The training of the archer in Japan at that time was severe. Even the many religious and court ceremonies surrounding kyujutsu had a definite air of the martial about them that was unmistakable. Shooting at multiple targets from atop a galloping horse, called *yabusame,* was the highlight of one such religious ceremony, which continues today as a popular tourist attraction in Japan. Kasagake was the ritual of riding and shooting at a hat mounted on a pole. The archer was also on horseback in the training method of *inumono,* the practice of shooting at dogs loosed in an arena.

Although the bow and arrow continued to be an important weapon of war in Japan until the beginning of the Edo period (around 1600), their use was thereafter eclipsed by the sword. The rigid and stringent training of earlier times gradually gave way to other forms of archery. Shooting competitively for distance became popular. There is a famous temple in Kyoto, the Sanjusangendo, which has a long corridor, about 131 yards long, along one side of the main structure, that became a favorite spot for archers to test themselves. The low eaves prevent an arrow released with any kind of an arc from reaching a target at the other end, so it was used as a proving ground for those who wished to see how far they could shoot an arrow with a flat trajectory. If you visit the Sanjusangendo, you can still see arrowheads bristling from the eaves from shots that went too high. Hitting the target was of secondary importance in these tests, as well as in those contests, also popular during the latter part of the feudal era, in which archers competed to see how many arrows they could launch, one after another, and have them all in flight simultaneously. *Kakemoto,* or the sport of shooting at targets that involves placing bets on the best shot, was another divergence from the true values of archery in Japan that furthered the decline of the art. Those who feel that the sideshow-type antics of karate's board-breaking contests and other such silliness degrade the martial arts will understand completely the words of Hinatsu Shigetaka who in 1716 noted that archery had devolved from an effective martial art into "mere gambling for the sake of amusement."

"If only those conversant in the ways of old would show us the etiquette and decorum of those earlier times," wrote Hinatsu, "nothing more important could be done to restore the true Way of the bow." What Hinatsu was decrying was not the loss of kyudo's purely martial applications, but the loss of kantoku.

Kantoku arose as a component of archery because so many of the ceremonies of the bow, although martial in flavor, were also conducted before the upper ranks of the samurai and the aristocratic classes. *Goshomatsu,* in fact, was the ritual of shooting arrows before an audience of the shogun himself, on New Year's Day. So kantoku was not just "grace under pressure." It was grace and calmness and elegant energy exercised properly under the very intense stress of performing before one's superiors. Kantoku disappeared from the art of archery in Japan when such ceremonies were replaced with sports and other shallow diversions, viewed by audiences unable or unwilling to discriminate the finer points of the art and preoccupied instead with the production of a "champion."

The contestant in any form of competition, from a sports championship to a music audition, is, I suppose, under some kind of pressure to perform well. But among the audiences for these competitions, how many are there who can perceive and distinguish real technique and virtuous behavior from mere artifice or displays of ego? How many spectators watching others perform under pressure can appreciate the attributes of kantoku that might be present in a given performer?

It is hard for us to imagine the sort of pressure the lords and masters brought to bear on the samurai in the days of feudalism, just as it was hard for me to comprehend the tension experienced by the practitioner of chado of that time who was engaged in making and serving tea before the nobility. But there are lessons to be learned from contemplating such things, for within the dynamics of those ancient pressures lies the essence of the quality of kantoku. Can we revive it?

Chapter Six

When the Nightingale Won't Sing

You meet a lot of different people in the dojo. Under the best of circumstances—if your dojo is a good and healthy one, I mean—the members of your training hall will be a fairly representative example of society. Everyone there seems to have his own motivations for training, his own unique ways of performing the techniques, and so on. As you spend more time around the dojo, however, you begin to sort out and classify various types of people. Take the attitudes your fellow dojo members display toward their training, for instance. After a while, you will note that these attitudes toward budo practice fall into roughly three categories, based on personalities I like to think of as the Hideyoshi, the Nobunaga, and the Tokugawa.

Do you recognize these names? You do if you know anything about Japanese history. Hideyoshi Toyotomi, Nobunaga Oda, and Tokugawa Ieyasu are the three most famous names in the military and political history of feudal Japan. They were the trio of great general warriors, shogun, who from the fourteenth through the sixteenth centuries sought to unify the many disparate fiefdoms of their country at different times, beginning with Nobunaga, then moving on to Hideyoshi, and finally to Tokugawa. If you are intrigued at all by the historical and cultural roots of the Japanese martial Ways, you should learn at least a little something about these three. A good way to start is to consider a poem, a bit of folk doggerel really, about the three shogun and a *hototogisu*. The hototogisu is a songbird of Japan, something like the European nightingale, and has a beautiful song. But in this poem, the hototogisu refuses to sing, and the writer describes the different approaches taken by Nobunaga, Hideyoshi, and Tokugawa to get the bird to sing. Once you hear the stanzas and learn something of the background of these three important men, I think you will understand why I categorize people's attitudes toward learning in the dojo as I do.

Oda Nobunaga, the eldest of the three (1532–1582), was, to put it mildly, a vicious tyrant. As a young general just starting out on his career, he sensed a weakness in the government of the reigning Ashikaga shogun. Like a wolf going after a weakened calf, Nobunaga attacked the shogun and overthrew his government. Because of his willingness to use both brute force and sheer intimidation against his enemies, Nobunaga's star continued to rise from that time on. Remember Darth Vader in the Star Wars movies? Nobunaga would have considered Mr. Vader a great role model.

Not surprisingly, Nobunaga gathered a number of allies around him who were awed by his cruel power or at least cowed into loyalty through a fear of him. But he acquired implacable enemies as well. Some were nearly as treacherous as he was. A few historians have suggested in retrospect that Nobunaga's despotic nature might be explainable as the desperately necessary actions of a man in extraordinarily difficult circumstances, and Nobunaga certainly was. But the overwhelmingly accepted portrait of the beady-eyed Nobunaga is one of a man utterly lacking in sensitivity or negotiating skills, one who got what he wanted by a tactless and brutal wielding of simple power and terror. Fittingly, he was assassinated by one of his own generals. In the poem about the hototogisu the lines regarding Oda Nobunaga go:

If the *hototogisu*
will not sing—
kill it.

Hideyoshi Toyotomi (1536–1598) was born into the peasant class of Japan and grew up to become a common soldier. Through luck, skill, and timing, he managed to rise through the ranks to become as influential a shogun as Japan has ever seen. A man like Hideyoshi could ascend to prominence in part because of the era in which he lived. During the latter half of the 1500s Japan was undergoing turbulent social uprisings. Farmers violently protested excessive taxes. Warfare was almost constant throughout much of the country. So there was ample opportunity for a samurai, even a low-ranked one like Hideyoshi, to prove himself on the field of battle. Hideyoshi was, further, a canny, brilliantly manipulative individual. He knew when to threaten or flatter; whatever it took to get what he wanted, Hideyoshi had an ability to do it, almost instinctively. He was phenomenally successful as a leader of men. He managed to unify a large part of Japan and keep it under his military control, even to the extent of marrying off his most trusted warriors and even his own family members to members of other families and clans to consolidate his structure of power.

Interestingly, the fine arts of Japan flourished dramatically under Hideyoshi's rule. Probably because he felt socially inferior to the samurai caste because of his own peasant roots, Hideyoshi pursued arts like the tea ceremony enthusiastically. He made elaborate attempts to ingratiate himself among true masters of the arts, but he was always vulgar and unrefined in his tastes, perhaps because he was more concerned with manipulating people than with actually learning from what they might teach him. The stanzas of the poem describing Hideyoshi say of him:

> If the *hototogisu*
>
> will not sing—
>
> try to make it sing.

The final great leader of old Japan was Tokugawa Ieyasu (1542–1616). If you have read the novel *Shogun* or seen the movie adapted from the book, you would recognize Tokugawa as the fictionalized character Toranaga. The Tokugawa family was a humble one (they stole their famous "hollyhock" crest from one of their own retainers). But they were ambitious. Ieyasu in particular displayed from his youth onward a remarkable perspicacity and a flair for taking command of any situation. He picked allies as well as he did enemies. He was a master strategist. As the leader of the Tokugawa clan, he suffered defeats, yet they were never so important as his victories.

In 1600 Tokugawa made a bid for control of virtually the whole country of Japan. It had been a dream for Nobunaga and Hideyoshi both, and both had come close. But it was Tokugawa who made the rule of the shogun sovereign throughout the land after he won the epic battle at Sekigahara. He founded a regime that lasted three hundred years. Tokugawa was farsighted, brave, and cunning. Above all, he was patient, always biding his time until the moment for action was exactly right, the odds in his favor. He never hurried; he was never idle. Of Tokugawa, the poem goes,

> If the *hototogisu*
> will not sing—
> wait.

Do you see what I mean when I say that the personalities you meet in a dojo can be categorized into the Nobunagas, the Hideyoshis, and the Tokugawas?

Chapter Seven

Not Yet, Not Yet

There is a story told among his senior students in the Japan Karate Association, that in 1957, when Gichin Funakoshi was eighty-nine years old, and only a few months before he died, he was talking at the dojo about karate technique. Making a fist and rotating his elbow, Funakoshi performed *soto ude uke,* the basic "outer forearm block." It is a movement that most of the karateka he was talking to had learned within the first few months of taking up the art. The outer block is just about as basic as karate basics can get. Funakoshi by that time had been performing the block for over seven decades. "I believe," he said, "I might finally be beginning to understand this movement."

I was told a similar story about the late Torao Mori, one of the great masters of kendo who taught in this country back in the 1960s. Mori was born in Japan and took up the Way of the sword when he was still a child. At that time, before World War II, kendo was often referred to by the name *gekken.* The term means literally "severe swordsmanship." At that time the practice of kendo was conducted under the tutelage of men who, in some cases, were old enough to have actually used a sword in life-and-death conflicts. Kendo practice then was rough, sometimes brutal by our standards. Yet central to the training was a constant emphasis on basics, simple movements performed over and over again, thousands of times in a single session. By the time Mori came to the United States, he was an expert with the bamboo sword. It is no exaggeration to say that his kendo was at a level without parallel outside of Japan, then or now. A friend of mine, a kendoka, told me that Mori had come to his university to lead a special training clinic at the kendo club there. My friend, like most American kendoka, held Mori in awe. So my friend was shocked when, warming up by himself early in the gym one morning during the clinic, he encountered Mori, who had arrived early as well. Mori asked if my friend would work with him for a while. "There is something I need to practice," Mori told my friend.

"Certainly, Sensei!" my friend answered, trying to conceal his delight. He supposed Mori had some high-level technique he was perfecting, perhaps the key to complete mastery of the art. It was an incredible opportunity for my friend, a private, one-on-one lesson with one of the senior kendo authorities in the world. They bowed, squared off, and then Mori asked if he might practice *shomen uchi*. My friend was sure he hadn't understood Mori correctly. Shomen uchi—striking to the front—is a simple vertical cut that every kendoka learns the first time he picks up a practice weapon.

"I still don't have it down right," Mori said.

I suspect that when young martial artists hear of these kinds of episodes they are skeptical. Beginners tend to be excited not about basics but about the more intricate "advanced" techniques or the more challenging kata. The typical karateka stands and pumps his fists back and forth, learning the straight punch as his teacher directs, but you may bet that from the corner of his eye he is watching the graceful leaping kicks of the senior black belts. Ask him which kata most concerns him, and invariably he will tell you it is the one that is just beyond the last one he has been taught. And so as he progresses up through the ranks he tends to look toward the acquisition of more techniques, more kata, seeing his training as a progression of knowledge. He judges his journey along the Way by how much he is acquiring along the trip.

But the budo, like all combative arts, are, by their nature, limited in curriculum and scope. There comes a time when the karateka, the aikidoka, or kendoka has been exposed to the full repertoire of the system. He is like a traveler who has explored every road and finds himself with only one destination, and that is back where he began. In this sense, the budo are circular. The last teaching is the first. The most esoteric secrets are to be found in the most basic of fundamentals. Mastery of the highest form can be described as an ability to return to the beginner's mind and spirit.

Ah ha! I can hear the clever reader exclaiming. If the budo are circular, if mastery is a matter of returning to the beginning, then isn't the beginner the same as a master? In some ways, perhaps that is true. There is a difference, though. The traveler who returns to his beginnings sees his hometown differently than a person who has never left it. He appreciates the food and the sights, all because he has seen much with which to compare his hometown. He experiences his beginnings through a wholly different perspective.

The expert budoka, too, comes home, in a manner of speaking, when he has nowhere else to go. Once he has been exposed to all the kata and the techniques and the strategies, he returns to the fundamentals of his art. Yet he is approaching those fundamentals with a perspective far wider and deeper than that of the neophyte. He realizes that those techniques and teachings he once wished to hurry through have a value that he can only now, as an expert, start to truly appreciate.

Coming back to where it was we started can be disappointing from one perspective. It appears to be contrary to our sense of progress. On the other hand, arriving back at the fundamentals is a destination to anticipate with some enjoyment. The circularity of the budo is a quality that makes them endlessly fascinating and infinitely challenging. There is always more to study, more to learn, in order to complete the journey. Perfection in the budo is circular; it is also an ever-expanding concept. Even the simplest technique is worth a lifetime of effort. Probably only near the end of that life, as Funakoshi must have discovered, do we begin to grasp the full significance of the techniques. We can never be satisfied. The Okinawan karate master Chosin Chibana put that sentiment well when, at the age of eighty when he was still practicing every day, he said, "When you reach the age of seventy or eighty, you must go on with your study with a positive attitude."

"And what constitutes a positive attitude?" one of his students asked him.

"Always thinking, 'not yet,'" Chibana told him, "not yet."

Chapter Eight

Budo Among the Blossoms

The Women's Association of the local Japan-America Society had asked to come to the dojo last summer to see a demonstration of the martial Ways. I was asked to do a flower arrangement for the *tokonoma,* the alcove at the front of the training hall. All traditional dojo have a place to display flowers, and although arranging the flowers is not a chore that is difficult for me normally, I was anxious about it. I knew some of the visitors who were coming were highly ranked in *ikebana,* or *kado* as it is also called, the Japanese art of flower arrangement, or the "flower Way." They would be critical of my arrangement, seeing any flaw, I was sure, and if my creation was a poor one, it would reflect badly on the dojo. So I began thinking about the task a couple of weeks ahead of time.

It may seem odd to be talking about the art of flower arranging in the context of the martial Ways. But actually, because the budo and kado are both traditional Japanese Ways, there are a number of parallels. Then, too, *uchi deshi* (private, usually live-in students of a teacher) must care for the training hall, so they are expected to have some skill at arranging flowers for the dojo alcove. These arrangements serve as both a memorial to the founder of whatever budo is being studied at that particular dojo and a reminder for the martial artist of the fragility of life.

An episode that occurred not too long after one of my karate sensei had come from Okinawa to attend graduate school in the United States might illustrate my point. My sensei was approached by a fellow who began extolling his own numerous accomplishments in karate. He had been his master's favorite pupil, he said, and he had been exposed to all the facets of the art. This fellow claimed that the master was planning to turn over the teaching and the care of the dojo completely to him very soon.

"Oh really," my sensei said, and innocently he asked, "What ryu, what school of flower arranging are you from?"

"Huh? Flower arranging? I do karate!"

From this man's point of view, the art of flower arranging was hardly compatible with his tough-guy karate image of himself. From my sensei's perspective, the skills of kado were indispensable to someone in charge of a dojo. A true uchi deshi would be an embarrassment to his teacher and a source of disdain for his training hall if he could not arrange the flowers in the tokonoma properly.

My own training in flower arrangement came from the wives of my various sensei and from my sensei themselves. It was a necessary art to learn, but I have to admit I did not think much more about arranging flowers at the alcove than I did about washing and sweeping the floor there. It was just another job for me to do. I hadn't given it much thought for many years, in fact, until that summer when I was given the chore of arranging the dojo's flowers for the demonstration.

You probably remember when you started to see the world through the eyes of the martial arts practitioner. You began to notice how people stand or walk, movements that make them vulnerable to this or that attack. You started to see the suki, the gaps in some people's sitting and standing postures, and how these people tend to go through life blindly in terms of their awareness and personal safety. The practice of your budo brought you new perspectives in this regard. In a similar but different way, the practice of kado brings the practitioner of the flower Way new perspectives. At least it did for me.

As I started thinking about the flowers I was supposed to put together for the demonstration, I found myself seeing through different eyes. One weekend I was out in the hills rock climbing. Hiking up to the cliffs and in between climbs I realized I was noticing the gnarled curves of the branch of an old maple. I was recalling all the lessons I had been taught about the correct compositions of branches and blossoms. Driving to the dojo one morning, soon afterward I suddenly saw flowers along the roadside, blue chicory, yellow yarrow, that I had overlooked day after day on the same trip. Just as budo training opened my eyes to the potential of danger and violence in life, faced with the task of putting together a floral display in an artistic way, I began to be aware of the beauty of plant life around me.

Because of the summer's heat and because my training in kado had stressed the use of naturally growing flowers of the season rather than those bought from or grown in a hothouse, it would not be a good idea to gather any of my flowers too far ahead of time. They would have wilted or died. It was not until I was actually driving to the dojo the morning of the demonstration that I put a *kama* (sickle) in the car so that I could use it when I jumped out along the way to cut some stalks of chicory, yarrow, and Queen Anne's lace that I saw beside the road. I used a rough-glazed tea bowl and arranged the flowers in the *nage-ire* style.

"Oh," said a woman examining my arrangement after the demonstration was over, "this is the style of kado where you just spontaneously 'drop in' the flowers to make the arrangement."

She was correct. "Nage-ire" means "dropped in," and that is the intended effect of the arrangement, spontaneous and informal. But I smiled to myself when I thought of all the planning and contemplation behind my "spontaneous" arrangement. In that way, too, the budo and kado are alike. The kicks and throws and strikes, the movements of the experienced budoka, these appear so natural and fluid it is hard to imagine all the painful and exacting work that went into their mastery. But in both the Way of flower arranging it is not the surface to which we must confine work that went into their mastery. But in both the Way of the martial artistourselves. To truly understand the budo, we must seek the profundities behind and beneath the surface and strive to grasp the lessons they offer in our lives every day.

Chapter Nine

Excess Baggage

"I would like to join your karate practice, but I wear glasses, you see, so could I possibly skip some of the rougher stuff?"

"I am interested in aikido, but I have very sensitive elbow joints from playing high school football. Could I ask, if I come to train, that the techniques you do that are applied against the elbows not be done on me?"

"I want to try kendo, but I don't think I'd get enough of a workout in a coed class. Do you have any classes with just men in them?"

Ask any budo teacher if these requests are familiar and he will nod. Then he will probably add one or two others he has heard. Questions of this nature are typical from prospective members of the dojo. Sometimes the requests are phrased in very polite, even timid ways. Other times the prospective student, assuming he has entered a place of business and therefore may demand more or less whatever kind of service he wants, will be forceful and emphatic in outlining his particular wishes. Then, too, there are would-be students who are clever and manipulative and who will attempt to smooth-talk their way into what they want. No matter what form these requests take, however, all of them are what we might think of as "excess baggage."

When a newcomer appears at the dojo door, he really doesn't need very much, if you come to think about it, to get him inside. He should be in reasonable physical and mental health and be willing to accept what he will encounter with an open mind. In reality, he needs almost nothing else. But in his own mind the new student often arrives believing he has a great many more necessities, and he will come schlepping up with them, even before his training has begun, toting them along like the excess baggage tourists carry with them on a holiday at the beach. The student carries this extra baggage because he has the very human notion that he is special in some way, that he has liabilities or considerations that others do not have. He feels he must, in all fairness, bring these to the attention of his teacher so that the teacher will be able to deal with them appropriately and effectively in class. Although the beginner is almost surely unaware of it, even at the onset of his training, even before he may have set foot onto the dojo floor, he has reached a critical stage in his education, one that is entirely up to his teacher to handle. The teacher has two choices. He can either listen patiently and explain that he will do everything possible to take the student's needs into consideration—or he can listen patiently and explain that in no way can the the dojo accommodate the excess baggage the student is carrying, and that, furthermore, believe it or not, the student will almost certainly be just fine without it.

If you encounter the sort of teacher who opts for the first approach, congratulations. You have found a cheap therapist who will reinforce all of your preconceptions about yourself. He will be sympathetic and understanding and accommodating. He will not challenge your sense of yourself, will never bring about a confrontation between you and your ego. If you run across a teacher who adopts the second kind of response, count your blessings. You may well have discovered a true sensei who can teach you things about yourself that you never knew.

The fact is, although your individual needs and shortcomings may seem very important to you, they are not really all that special. Chances are, if you can walk into a dojo under your own power, you are in good enough shape to begin training there. Of course, your asthma or your myopia or lack of flexibility may be a problem. But if you had the opportunity to ask her, you would probably discover that the woman practicing beside you is dealing with chronic arthritis. The man on the other side has a left hip that has a slight congenital deformity, and the girl behind you suffers from chronic bronchitis. And it's very likely that they all began their training by thinking *their* problems were as special as yours.

Another pertinent fact is that a principal attribute of the martial Ways, one of their greatest assets as paths of self-discovery and personal growth, is their breadth. Karate, judo, kendo, and aikido were not meant just for the Japanese. Or just for men. Or just for finely conditioned athletes. Unlike the classical warrior arts that preceded them in old Japan and that were confined in their scope and availability to the samurai caste, the budo have a much wider aim. They were meant for *everyone*. And, by their nature, when they are taught, no special consideration may be given to *anyone*.

Got a bad right knee? Then your kicks with that leg may not be as strong as mine. I've got an injury-weakened left shoulder, so my strikes on that side might not be as powerful as yours. But when our sensei counts off the kicks, you must be trying your best to kick even if those kicks are not as good as mine. When punching, I have to do the same, give it my complete effort even if my best isn't going to be the same as yours. And neither you nor I can do our best when we're carrying excess baggage.

If you ever have an opportunity to attend a traditional ceremony of tea, or *chado,* you should take it, for many reasons. There are a number of lessons for the budoka to learn in the confines of the tea hut. Even entering the hut itself provides insight in the Way. In a properly built *chashitsu,* as a tea hut is called in Japanese, there is a peculiar kind of doorway, one that was designed by the great tea master Sen no Rikyu. As I have mentioned before, this door is called a *nijiri guchi,* which means roughly a "crawling in space." To the uninitiated, the nijiri guchi might be mistaken for a little window. It is only a few feet square. Anyone wishing to enter, to participate in the tea ceremony, must pass through this little door by lowering himself and nearly crawling through the small passage.

The history of the nijiri guchi is informative. Sen no Rikyu's most famous pupil in the Way of tea was Toyotomi Hideyoshi, the fierce warlord who ruled much of Japan during the latter half of the sixteenth century. Hideyoshi was passionate about the tea ceremony. He saw in its sober and refined elegance a goal he desperately pursued. But with Hideyoshi, it was always an inner battle between his wish for the simple beauty that he knew marked a true connoisseur, and his fevered and ambitious ego. He knew in his heart that in the quiet simplicity of the tea hut was an aesthetic to be treasured. Yet it was difficult for him to give up the magnificent clothes and the fabulously expensive swords he wore, the trappings of his status as a shogun. He identified his position with these things, and he did not wish to be without them. (He was no different, really from the prospective students we are talking about, those who identify themselves so closely with their own things or ideas or preconceptions or problems.) According to the traditions of the tea ceremony, Sen no Rikyu devised the nijiri guchi so that if the haughty Hideyoshi wished to enter sincerely into the spirit of tea, he would have to humble himself and crawl through the door. This architectural feature of the tea ceremony remains to this day. The tea house door is open to all. But there is only one way to enter. No exceptions can be made, regardless of one's station or circumstances in life.

The door to the dojo is different in appearance, true, but it is very similar to the tea house's nijiri guchi. There is room only for you to come in. You must leave your excess baggage outside. Trust me. Trust your teacher. Whatever you leave behind, you will not miss it at all.

Chapter Ten

A Snowflake on a Hot Stove

I was once invited to speak to a university's religious studies class about the role of the martial Ways in Japanese culture and society. My talk was preceded by a film on kendo, the Way of the sword. After my lecture, one of the students asked me about what he'd seen in the film.

"In one of those kendo tournament matches, the referee called a halt to the action," he said. "But when one guy turned away to go back to his starting place, the other one hit him in the back of the head."

This sometimes happens in kendo matches, for a couple of reasons. First, sometimes in a contest a participant is at such a high level of fighting spirit that he may strike reflexively when an obvious target is presented to him. It's not even a conscious act. Another reason for such a hit is that to turn one's back on an opponent is a gross insult in the budo. It is like saying, "You're so inept that I can turn away from you without fear of injury." Even if it is unintentional, turning your back on an opponent is a breach of etiquette that will rarely go unanswered by a more skilled martial artist.

"What I noticed," the student went on, "was that the guy who was hit didn't react to it at all. He just turned back around, bowed, and the match went on. If that had happened in the United States, the typical American athlete would have punched out the guy who sucker struck him. He'd have lost his temper."

A good point. There are marked contrasts in the way in which a Japanese and an American are likely to react to provocation. The former often seems to have some kind of Buddha-like serenity in the face of irritation (or so it seems, anyway), while an average American is typically quick to respond with as much if not more ire than that which was directed against him. (We are speaking here, of course, in gross generalities. There are plenty of exceptions, for instances, the train conductor I encountered in Yokohama once who was literally screaming in my face because he insisted—wrongly it turned out—that my rail pass was not valid on a local line. And I have seen police officers in New Orleans during Mardi Gras faced with the most outrageous, potentially violent, and nerve-wracking confrontations with crowds, yet the officers were so imperturbable you'd have thought they were going to nod off on a nap at any moment.)

It is interesting and worthwhile to note that those traits seem to flip-flop when you compare not individuals, but entire nations. Japan is extremely sensitive to criticism and protests energetically any adverse comments from the rest of the world about any of its governmental policies. America not only patiently endures the streams of international invectives thrown at it; the country's propensity for self-criticism is sometimes so extreme that it is absurd.

But bearing in mind that we are speaking in generalities, what is it about the cool, almost arctic temperament of the average Japanese and the fiery, quick-to-anger disposition of so many Americans? One clue might be found in the differing perceptions each has of what constitutes control: control of oneself as well as control of others. Let us say, for instance, that you are involved in a long and frustrating business negotiation with a representative of another firm. The discussion seems hopelessly deadlocked. Irritation levels are into the red zone.

"Look," you finally say, rather loudly and with a definite note of exasperation in your voice, "you have our final offer. So let's fish or, damn it, cut bait!"

To most Americans, this kind of take-charge attitude is indicative of a power play. By speaking forcefully, angrily even, you have demonstrated that you are tired of fooling around. You are taking control of the situation. To many Japanese, though, your reaction to the stalled discussion is a sure sign that you have just relinquished control of the situation. Those Japanese, would believe that your negotiating opponent has just won a major advantage by forcing you to lose your temper and reveal your inner feelings. They would conclude that your opponent now knows much more about you and your intentions than you do about him and his. Control of others, to the Japanese mind, invariably begins with control of one's self. By sitting quietly in the negotiating session, revealing no emotion, your opponent manipulated you into a temper tantrum and unbalanced you psychologically.

I want to clarify again that we are speaking in the broadest of cultural tones. Individual temperament, too, plays a role here, obviously. Still Japanese culture, like the cultures of much of the rest of the East (and they may thank Confucius for this; the emphasis in his philosophy on self-control had a powerful impact on societies throughout Asia) celebrates emotional equanimity and the spirit of imperturbability. It is hardly surprising that in the Japanese martial disciplines, a reflection after all, of Japanese culture, such a mentality would figure so predominantly. Self-control and impassivity in the face of provocation was not just a matter of style for the samurai. It was a strategy. For battle. For relationships with others. For life.

One warrior of the classical age in Japan who exemplified self-control was Takeda Shingen, who, along with his rival Uyesugi Kenshin, dominated much of central Japan during the middle part of the sixteenth century. Takeda and Kenshin met in a series of battles. Both were military geniuses and neither was ever able to conclusively defeat the other. According to a popular legend that may or may not have a basis in fact, in one of their most furious battles, Kenshin became impatient with his army's inability to rout Takeda's troops from the field. Kenshin was as famous for his impetuousness as he was for his brilliant tactics. Without warning, he leaped on his horse and rode right through the lines. His action was impulsive and so utterly unexpected that he made it into the camp of the Takeda general unchallenged. Kenshin jumped off his mount and drew his sword, catching Takeda, who was still sitting on a camp stool, by surprise. Kenshin raised his weapon and held it above Takeda's head. "What would you say now?" he asked Takeda. Directly confronting this unexpected brush with death, Takeda composed a poem. With perfect calm, he answered, "A flake of snow on a blazing stove." He reached up and tapped Kenshin's sword with his iron fan. Kenshin, in admiration of his foe's self-control, resheathed his weapon and rode away.

The spirit exemplified by Takeda has survived and is still admired today in the modern Japanese budo. To control oneself in times of stress is vital. It is more important than being skillful or brave or successful in strategy. Back in the 1960's, for example, it was not unusual for karateka or judoka to be disqualified during tournaments because they became visibly angry at a referee's decision. Their disqualification was sometimes misinterpreted as a punishment for bad behavior. The real reason they were eliminated was becouse of the recognition that if the contest had been real, if it had been a true fight to the death, a loss of self-control would almost surely be just the advantage an enemy would need to make the kill or make the victory.

I have a feeling that the Japanese kendoka who got smacked on the back of the head was just as angry, just as frustrated as certain tennis players we've seen on the professional circuit who know their serve was in but the linesmen called it out. But whereas some of these players scream and throw fits, the kendoka shows absolutely nothing. These tennis players are venting their emotions and simultaneously hoping to intimidate the officials, trying to gain a measure of control over them for future line calls. Conversely, the kendoka is internalizing his emotion and simultaneously seeking to intimidate his opponent, saying in effect, "No matter how you antagonize me, you cannot unsettle my equanimity. My inner self is still serene, and with that advantage I am going to beat you."

Most of us have a lot of practice at showing our anger by shouting, eyes ablaze, faces crimson with rage. What we need to learn from the budo is another way to display our emotions, by redirecting them inward, by controlling and channelling them so they cannot be detected visibly. Instead of venting anger, we can use it as a weapon. And like most effective weapons, it is best kept hidden until needed.

Chapter Eleven

The Sound of the Drum

> Masters are usually indistinguishable from the rest of the
> people until they are required to express themselves through
> their creations, just as a drum is made to produce sound that
> varies according to the degree of strength applied to the beater.
>
> —Michiji Ishikawa

The concept of the master is a foreign one to most of us in the West, in
this century at least. Connotations of the word conjure up elements of feudalism (a system of government and living that Americans in particular have
never experienced at all) or the slave plantations (which we did experience
and are the worse for it, in so many ways). We have not, since the Industrial
Revolution, thought much about masters in terms of arts or artisanship.
Most of us, face it, just don't spend much time around people we would
think of as masters at anything, masters of any sort. An exception to that
would be the martial arts, if the listings in the Yellow Pages of any city of
any size are any indication. Thumb through the section of the phone book
devoted to martial arts and you may conclude that there are about five masters to the square mile in some places. And they're clustered more thickly in
other places. Contrary to Professor Ichikawa's description of a master, most
of the masters you are likely to be introduced to through their advertisements in the phone book and elsewhere are not exactly what you would call
"indistinguishable." Typically, their training uniforms are bedecked with

stripes, patches, and embroidery. Many of them are the sort of people who will happily announce their status as masters at every opportunity, printing their title on their business cards, on their stationery, and so on.

Ofttimes when I see someone who is advertising himself as a master martial artist I am reminded of a budo master whose student told me a tale that began at the end of World War II in Japan. The master ran an electric fan factory the size of a suburban home garage in the old Sumida district of Tokyo. Above the factory was his house. Behind the factory was a small dojo where he taught a classical method of using the sword. His membership was small, no more than a dozen students. In 1944 all that came to an end. The building housing the factory and his home above it and the dojo were burned to the ground in an Allied air raid. Also gone were all the master's belongings, his clothes and appliances and furniture, and gone, too, were precious instructional scrolls and other artifacts he had inherited from his teacher. The master's heartaches were significant ones, cares shared by many hundreds of thousands of people in Japan at that time, but his troubles were far from over. His wife died of pneumonia. He received word less than a month later that his only son had been killed in action in Manchuria. The master was living under a piece of corrugated tin, out in the open, at the time he got that news. He had no income, only a few clothes, and nothing to eat but what was contributed to him by neighbors and his students.

"And then," his student told me, "a fire destroyed everything that remained in an area of several blocks all around the master's neighborhood. It was right after Japan's surrender. There was utter chaos. The police and community government were unsure of their authority." It was, you can imagine, much like the disaster of Kobe, Japan, in the mid-1990s, like the earthquakes or other such massive tragedies that befall places from time to time.

"In that mess, the neighborhood turned to my teacher" the student told me. "He was a respected businessman, after all. And he was a budo sensei. That meant that people looked up to him." The master responded by organizing his neighbors into various committees. Some were given the task of making shelters. Others were sent to collect and disperse food. The master led the effort to bring his community through the crisis, even in the midst of his personal grief. During the Occupation he oversaw the eventual rebuilding of that part of the Sumida district. He was elected president of his ward in the first elections of the postwar era, a position he held for over a decade.

That master never had any glitzy uniforms. He certainly did not have stationery or business cards with "MASTER" printed on them. There was really no need for anything like that. He demonstrated his mastery quite convincingly when the time came for him to do so. When the drum was hit, hit hard, it responded with a clear, deep, and loud sound. I wonder, if they were hit as hard as that master was, what the sound would be from all those masters listed in the Yellow Pages?

Chapter Twelve

Sottaku Doji

In the Zen treatise the *Hekigan Roku (The Blue Cliff Record)* is found the expression *"sottaku doji."* Sottaku means "a pecking noise." *Doji* means "simultaneously." In ordinary conversation sottaku doji refers to the reaction that occurs between a mother bird and her chicks that are about to hatch. When it is still in the egg but ready to come out, the chick begins to make tentative pecks against the inside of its shell. Could there be a smaller sound in the universe? And yet the mother bird hears it. She responds, pecking on the outside of the shell to assist the hatchling in its struggle to be born.

The expression "sottaku doji" appears in the *Blue Cliff Record* for the same reason one hears of it in many of the traditional arts of Japan, including the budo—because it refers to the unique relationship between a teacher and his student. The other day I saw a book purporting to "teach the reader Zen" without the assistance of a Zen master. I wish good luck to its readers, as well as to those readers of books or viewers of videotapes who think they can learn martial arts from them. I don't think they will get very far. A competent teacher is absolutely mandatory for getting yourself on the path of Zen or the budo. You need teacher's guiding hand to lead you along all but the most abbreviated stretches of the journey.

The search for a master or even a good teacher can be a monumental task. Yet once you have completed the search, once you have found someone you can trust to guide you, it is a mistake for you to assume that your travails are over and the trip is going to be a smooth and uneventful one.

For months, for close to a year, I had been struggling with a kata that my karate sensei had given me. Among its final movements was a big jump that spun the body around dramatically in midair. At least that is what it was supposed to do. In my case, the amazing leap was more like an arthritic stumble. I fell too many times to remember. And just when I was feeling as clumsy as I thought possible, my sensei would demonstrate, and his leap would be spectacular and effortless. It was maddening.

I had learned the movements of the kata in the autumn, spent a winter bouncing off the cold wooden floor of the dojo, and as soon as spring came I was outside working on the jump on the damp ground. I perspired through a wickedly hot summer, still at it, and with August upon me I still had little to show for my efforts.

"Shift your weight to your front leg before you jump," Sensei finally said to me one day, matter-of-factly. I did. And I jumped. And I seemed to soar. I sailed into the air like I had wings, rotated perfectly, and landed without a sound, solidly. Well, perhaps my memory has exaggerated it a bit. But I did have a terrific breakthrough that day. It was like being given the key to a door I had been trying to batter down. It was such a joyful experience I kept at it for nearly half an hour before it occurred to me what my sensei had done. A single sentence had lifted the weight of nearly a year of frustration and failed effort. And it was so simple, just a shift in weight made all the difference.

I was so angry at my sensei I could hardly see straight.

"He could have saved me so much time!" I complained to his wife. "Why didn't he tell me that months ago?" She listened to my rantings without comment, allowing me to vent some of my crankiness.

"Would you have heard him if he had told you months ago?" she finally asked me.

As I thought about it, I realized that no, I would not have been likely to have heard my sensei's advice before. Oh, I might have heard the words he used. But my body would not have been able to translate those words into physical action. Sensei knew this, and he knew exactly when the time was right to give me what I needed. This is the meaning—for the budoka at least—of sottaku doji.

To be started on the road of the martial Way is not the same as seeing the entire journey laid out before you. There are numerous obstacles, many of them far too difficult for the beginner or even the more advanced student to try to surmount before he is ready. This is where the teacher comes in. A sensei leads, but at times he sits and watches and waits while the student struggles, giving a little push at just the crucial moment it is needed.

Obviously, the practitioner of a budo who is in a class with dozens of others, all of whom are learning the same kata or techniques at the same, pre-arranged time, will never experience sottaku doji. Too much of the modern budo, conducted en masse in gymnasium-like halls, is more an assembly-line process than anything remotely connected with the creation of an art. Over the roar of commercialism that sounds in places like this, the teacher is quite oblivious to the hesitant peck of the student in need of hatching. Sottaku doji demands the quiet, the intimacy of a special and personal relationship between the sensei and his student. Without it, one must wonder how the student can ever grow and mature or how the teacher can ever hope to successfully reproduce himself.

Chapter Thirteen

Enzan O Metsuke
("Viewing the Distant Mountain")

Kyoboku kazeoshi. (The taller the tree, the stronger
the wind that pushes against it.)

—Japanese proverb

In 1933 Gichin Funakoshi faced a quandary of the sort you would imagine only a scholar or some linguist would worry over. It was a matter so trivial that unless you can read Japanese it would barely make any sense at all,
and even if you could, you might be tempted to wonder what the fuss was
all about. Specifically, the dilemma Funakoshi, the father of Japanese karate,
faced was exactly what characters he would choose in writing the word
"karate."

As every budoka knows, it was Funakoshi who brought the native
Okinawan art of karate to mainland Japan. Realizing that because karate was
both a ferocious fighting art and one of Okinawan origin (and therefore
considered gauche and common in the extreme by the average Japanese),
Funakoshi knew his karate would have two strikes against it right from the
start. So he concentrated on disseminating karate among the more educat-
ed and influential of Japanese society. During the first five years Funakoshi
was in Japan he exhibited karate almost exclusively to professional groups
and at universities. One school that was immediately impressed with the art

was the prestigious Keio University in Tokyo. In 1924 Keio asked Funakoshi to start the first collegiate karate club in Japan. In addition to instruction, Funakoshi also formed a group of university karateka devoted to a technical and philosophical study of the Okinawan art. During a meeting of this group he formally introduced an idea he had formulated and developed privately over several years.

Many Okinawans believed that their fighting art, which we today know by the name of karate, had originated almost entirely from outside, Chinese sources. They had always credited China's parentage of the art, and that is why it was known as *Tode*. *To* was an Okinawan pronunciation of the word for the country of T'ang, or China (pronounced *kara* in Japanese). *De* was an Okinawan pronunciation of the Japanese word *te,* meaning "hand." So tode was the "China hand art." Funakoshi disagreed with the thought behind this choice of names. He reasoned that karate was an art that may have been influenced by the fighting arts of China, but many of its techniques and strategies were purely of Okinawan heritage, unique to the island kingdom. He proposed the notion that a more appropriate name for the art of tode would be karate (which the art was already sometimes called, and which was a term that had been in use for many, many years on Okinawa), and that further the word denoting China's contributions to the art should be abandoned and replaced with kara, or "empty."

Funakoshi's logic was sound and operated on many levels. He observed that karate was, indeed, the Way of the empty hand, relying on no other weapons than the natural ones of the body. He related the metaphysical emptiness of karate with the "emptiness" of Buddhist philosophy, and this connection serves to remind us that at the center of the budo is the concept of the Void. He was fond of quoting the Pure Heart Sutra of Buddhism, the *Hannya Shin-gyo,* which instructs that "in form there is emptiness; in emptiness there is form." Finally, he maintained that giving karate the appropriate characters in writing would restore a proper recognition of the Okinawan contribution to the art, putting the emphasis where he believed it belonged.

(It is only fair to tell you that this account is grossly simplified. There were a number of political and social forces working in Japan at that time, and it would be ridiculous to imagine that Funakoshi was immune to them. Japan, for instance, had invaded China at the time. There was considerable anti-Chinese sentiment among Japanese, and surely Funakoshi must have taken this into account when he brought up the idea of changing the name.)

The karate study group at Keio University supported Funakoshi's proposition to change the name of the art to karate, and soon after he published a letter on the subject in a Tokyo newspaper. In typically phlegmatic words, Funakoshi was later to recall that his "suggestion elicited violent outbursts of criticism in Tokyo and Okinawa." To say the least. The "violent outbursts" were, in part, a series of angry letters from a number of karateka, especially those still in Okinawa, that fairly reeked with insulting innuendo and with implied threats. Funakoshi faced a withering barrage of criticism. And more. During the months following the publication of his letter Funakoshi was visited by some challengers who were deadly serious. He also had to contend with some thugs who were hired to beat or even kill him. When one of Funakoshi's most senior students from this era was asked many years later what the outcome of these challenges was, he replied, "Well, the name of karate stayed changed as Funakoshi wanted it."

We can speculate, but I do not know what prompted Funakoshi to make the calligraphic changes, since he must have been mindful of the furor his suggestion would create. I do not know how he felt about taking the brunt of such bitter and at times dangerous criticism. But if I had to guess, I would say he sustained himself by focusing his vision in the manner of *enzan o metsuke*—"viewing the distant mountain."

Enzan o metsuke is a bit of technical advice that is often imparted to students of the budo. It pertains to the question of where you are supposed to fasten your gaze when facing an opponent. One strategy calls for staring slightly beyond the shoulders of the opponent, as if looking at a mountain in the far distance. This allows the sight to be centered on nothing in particular, taking in all movement. But enzan o metsuke also encompasses the mental process of putting matters into a more far-reaching perspective than that of the immediate present, to see the events in one's life as they will figure not right now, not tomorrow, but in the distant future.

Readers who have recently graduated from school may have an idea of what this aspect of enzan o metsuke is all about, particularly if they can remember back to the year before your graduation. Only a couple of semesters to go, but suddenly the time seemed like forever. At that moment it would have been easy to call it quits. Many do. In the same way and for the same reason, the highest dropout rate in the average budo dojo comes at the time when the student is preparing for the first grade of black belt. But the disciplined budoka, who is capable of looking into his future, like the well-motivated high school or college student, can hang in there until he has reached his goal. He knows that often the greater the obstacle, the greater will be the rewards when the roadblocks have finally been overcome.

Maybe that is what brought Funakoshi through the trying times of 1933, a belief that in the future karate would benefit from his contribution. It has. Today karateka seek the profound meanings of the emptiness that is implied by the character *kara,* and they try to find within themselves the realization of the concept. By changing karate from "China hand" to "empty hand," Funakoshi took a major step in elevating karate to the status of a respected budo in Japan.

Even constructive criticism is hard medicine. I have received constructive feedback about things I have written, and I have also been on the receiving end of criticism that was pointless and hurtful and unearned. You must have had your own encounters with this sort of attack. Even if you know that such baseless criticism is pointless and says more about those criticizing you than it does about you, you would have to be a callous person not to be hurt and discouraged by such attacks. When I find myself in such a situation I think about how we in the budo are fortunate to have examples like Gichin Funakoshi. Although few of us will make his kind of contributions, it is comforting to remember that he had to put up with his share of adversity, criticism, and frustration. He endured it by focusing his attention on the ultimate outcome of his actions and by holding on to the sincere belief that he was doing what was right. He set his gaze not upon the immediate moment but on the eventual culmination of what it was he sought to do. As we should learn to do when faced with the same kinds of problems, Funakoshi adopted the long-distance vision of enzan o metsuke.

Chapter Fourteen

Jikishin ("Direct Mind")

In the city of Kyoto in Japan, there is a small *chaseki,* a single-room hut used for the tea ceremony, that was built by the seventeenth-century warrior and tea master Furuta Oribe. As with most huts of its kind, one corner of the room is given to an alcove where flowers and a scroll of calligraphy are usually displayed. The scrolls are changed regularly, with the changing of the seasons. But according to one of his students, Oribe's favorite scroll for hanging in his tea hut read simply *Jikishin kore dojo*—*"Jiki*-mind is the place to practice."

Jikishin. Jiki-mind. Unlike many words or concepts that we come across in our training that have recondite meanings and shades of nuance that are difficult to penetrate, *jiki* is quite simple and straightforward. It means "directly," or "immediately," or "without delay." The phrase "Jikishin kore dojo," so appealing to a person of martial and aesthetic tendencies, occurs frequently in the context of explaining the traditional Japanese disciplines. Two schools of martial arts—the ancient Jikishinkage ryu of swordsmanship and the distantly related Jikishinkage ryu of the *naginata*—include the word "jiki" in their names.

The translation of "jiki" might be basic; its meaning for the budoka, however, is not so easily grasped. To begin to appreciate its wider significance first we need to consider for a moment the manner in which most of us experience the world around us, day to day. Obviously, the way we spend our waking hours is far different from the way our early ancestors spent theirs. Early man's experience with the world tended to be direct and immediate, no doubt about it. If he was hungry he went out looking for something to impale with his spear and bring home for dinner, or he grubbed his day's sustenance from the earth. Even as recently as a century ago, the forefathers of many of us butchered their own livestock and harvested their own crops. But today we rarely see food that has not been processed in some way and wrapped in plastic. This important distinction in the way we relate to the world as compared with the way our ancestors did can be seen in a variety of our cultural and personal practices. We do not bury our own dead; rarely do women today have children without the attendance of a doctor and the administering of medications that distance the mother from the immediacy of the act of bearing a child. In short, people today live life, an awful lot of it anyway, filtered through all sorts of contrived or artificial mediums. (I'm not complaining about this, mind you. I'm very happy I didn't have to catch the cod I ate last night, even more delighted that my wife had assistance in delivering our child a few years ago. But the point remains that we live without much of the direct, immediate experiences that were an everyday fact of life for our ancestors.)

These filters on our routine experience carry over into the way men and women in our century organize their thought processes. If a predator, a lion with an empty belly say, appeared at the entrance to his shelter, early man had little use for philosophy and did not rationalize about it. He reacted instantly, grabbing whatever weapon was handy, and took care of business. If he was slow and thought too much about what to do, he would find himself the cat's main course, and that would be that. America's pioneers faced an environment nearly equally as hostile, in an equally direct and simple way. Yet in our age the dangers and challenges we meet are almost always of a different sort entirely. The threats we encounter are no less serious, but they come in the form of lawsuits and legal actions or financial crises. And rarely do we confront them ourselves. Once again we have intermediaries; lawyers, accountants, and politicians do it for us.

Despite some drawbacks, there isn't much doubt that our ways of dealing with problems are more sensible, given the structure of modern society. If someone hits your car, it is better to sue him for damages rather than run him through with a sword and pillage his home to gain recompense. (It would probably make us feel better, I'm not denying that. But working through the legal system is not quite so messy.) But if we become too dependent on all the intermediaries and filters, we can lose something valuable in ourselves. We risk losing the ability to act and react as directly and immediately as our ancestors did. To gain some idea of what I mean, one need only observe the reactions of a student in a budo dojo the very first time he is "attacked" in even a remotely realistic fashion. He may have been dealing technically with the same attack for months. It has always been launched at him slowly, with prior warning, always accompanied by the instructions of the teacher. The student has always had time to think, to reflect, to rationalize about the proper response he needs to make. And then invariably, sooner or later, a senior or a teacher will unleash a strike for which there is no warning, no prior instruction. It is a moment of absolute intensity. There can be no analysis, no thinking at all about what to do. All the "filters" are gone. The reaction must be visceral and instant. The reaction must be not all that different from the reactions of the Neanderthal facing that gluttonous lion at his front door.

In the great majority of these cases, the first time a student is confronted with an attack that is direct and apparently spontaneous and serious, the student will crumble in one of several different ways. Some students will jump back or offer the most frantic and ineffective of parries. Quite soon after that, a student's thoughts will begin to arrange themselves into all kinds of rationalizations. "I need more practice." "That wasn't fair, I wasn't ready." "It wouldn't have happened that way out on the street." The excuses run on and on in the mind of the student who has failed in the face of the first "real" attack. All of his rationalizations may be accurate ones. Or they may be utter nonsense. But all of them, accurate or not, are immaterial in the context of the budo. In the dojo, an attack or a response succeeds or fails. That's it. There is no need, no place, for excuses, no matter how relevant they may be. We cannot dodge those confrontations or rely on an intermediary to shield us from them. Nor can we "explain" our responses away. We can only meet each attack directly, honestly, without hesitation. We have no choice but to respond with jikishin. The direct mind.

So you see, or should by now, why so little explanation is given during some phases of training and instead budoka are encouraged to move without conscious thought. In court, the lawyer may succeed by clever rhetoric. The businessman may prevail in a negotiation by using careful economic analysis that gives him an edge. The scientist advances through study and deliberation. But when any of these individuals comes to the dojo, his respective approaches to thinking go right out the window. In the dojo, as we are reminded by the calligraphy hanging in Oribe's tea house, the "direct mind is the place to practice."

Chapter Fifteen

Swimming 'Round the Stone

Every spring in old Japan, on the fifth day of the fifth month, the parents of boys would decorate their homes with long banners, sewn in the shape of carp and fixed to tall bamboo poles. The carp would "swim" in the breeze, one carp for each male child in the house. These *koinobori* (literally "carp flags") are still popular adornments for houses on the fifth day of May in modern Japan. But the times being what they are, banners are now hung for every child in the house, male or female. In Japanese culture the carp has a long history of respect because many of its attributes have been considered worthy of emulation. The carp has also been considered a paragon of bravery. As you may know if you have ever snagged one while fishing, the carp will fight furiously, thrashing and leaping from the water in its struggle to get free. When the battle has been lost, however, and the fish is on the cutting board and ready to be dispatched, it lies quietly, accepting its fate with complete composure and stoicism, perfectly in the spirit with which the samurai sought to face his own death.

The Japanese may have venerated the spirit of the carp, but it was from the Chinese that they learned to selectively breed the fish, bringing out the best colors and elongating the carp's fins into shapes that drape and float beautifully as the fish swim about. Chinese experts on carp breeding imparted many of their secrets to the Japanese several centuries ago, and as a result in Japan today the raising of carp or *koi,* is a multimillion-yen business, with a single perfect specimen selling for far more than the cost of a new luxury car.

One technique for raising healthy fish that the Japanese learned from the Chinese was to put a stone into the pond where the fish lived. If the koi is placed in a pond with nothing but water, the Chinese knew, the fish will become lazy and listless and subject to disease. Place a stone in that same pond, and in swimming about it the koi will tend to grow energetic and strong. I sometimes think the budo are like that. They are a stone, of sorts, for those of us who have made the martial Ways a part of our lives.

There has been a great deal in the media extolling the benefits of the martial Ways for children. Nearly all of this information comes from people who know more about both children and the budo than do I. I can only speak from the limits of my own experience, having started my own practice of these arts before I was a teenager. I cannot say that the Japanese martial disciplines worked any miracles in my own childhood. There were no threatening bullies in my neighborhood whom I finally faced down in a climactic schoolyard battle. There was no dramatic denouement in my budo practice when I won both the big tournament and the heart of the beautiful blonde girl at the same time. (I grew up in southwest Missouri with its predominant genetic breed of Scots-Irish; we didn't even have any blondes.) Instead, I think the principal benefit of my martial arts training was more subtle, so much so that it was a long time after my childhood that I even began to think of how my training had affected me.

All of this came to mind when I was listening to a discussion of the problems faced by young people today: drugs, fractured families, teen pregnancy, suicide; it was a rather chaotic and depressing portrait of adolescence. It seems this is not a particularly swell time to be a teenager. But then again the period when I went through adolescence, the 1960s, was not exactly a Norman Rockwell idyll. Drugs and alcohol were a scourge back then (except that drugs were still viewed as chic, and there was no group like Students Against Drunk Driving to tell the other side of the story about excessive drinking). The 1960s had their own social problems. On more than one occasion I had to be careful getting to the university judo club where I trained because antiwar demonstrations were rocking the campus and violence in the pursuit of "peace" was not uncommon. I remember once, as a skinny high school sophomore I found myself temporarily in the midst of a Black Panther rally. I wasn't demanding any capitulation from the university; I was just trying to get to the dojo to practice my forward rolls.

My point is that although their experiences may differ in kind and intensity, adolescents in any time in history are forced to confront some difficult, seemingly overwhelming obstacles. And just as some young budoka now are trying to use lessons learned in the dojo to navigate their way through those obstacles, when I was that age my involvement in the budo helped me avoid a lot of pitfalls into which others around me fell.

It was not the techniques or the kata or the severity of the training that was so beneficial to me as a young person. The unerring compass point that the budo provided in my life was *consistency*. In a world where values were turned upside down, where fashions came and went from love beads to psychedelic underwear, the budo were steadfast. For me and for others who regularly attended training there, the dojo had the consistency of a granite boulder. The budo were the stone around which we swam. The etiquette, the methods, the challenges—all were the same for us as they had been for my teachers and for their teachers before them. Outside its walls the storms of social change raged and ebbed, but inside the dojo was the calm of a temple. We always knew the stone was there and we could depend on it.

In this sense the budo were something timeless for those of us who followed them as youngsters living in an era when it was easy to become wrapped up in the rapid pace of events unfolding all around us. The budo taught that our bell-bottom pants and long hair might be replaced by peglegs and crewcuts according to the next dictate of fashion, but the values of

self-discipline, concern and respect for others, and the long-term commitment required by judo, karate, kendo, and the other martial Ways were here
to stay. They were important. They were a core on which to center our lives.
Further, although we had the opportunity and were encouraged to experiment and test the limits of freedom in the 1960s, we knew that freedom
had limits that could not be messed with. The testing ended at the door of
the dojo. This was a lesson that has stayed with many of us who began our
journey on the martial Ways during that decade. As adults now, we understand what we learned then, that while one can be open to change and to
new opportunities, there are other constants that should not be so lightly
discarded.

No doubt some readers will take exception to these observations.
Currently it is considered progressive to "take what is useful" from the training hall and discard whatever else one feels is unessential, unimportant, or
just uninteresting according to the times. I wonder, though, if what is
important to those who advocate this approach will be important to future
students a couple of decades from now. I wonder, if they reject the legacy
that has been passed on for generations and that formed a compass for my
life and the lives of many of my fellow budoka, what will they replace it
with. I wonder what stone they will swim around.

Chapter Sixteen

Ichi-go, Ichi-e
("One Encounter, One Chance")

In the era of Kanbun, which in the West covered the years from 1661 to 1673, Yamada Asayemon Sadatake was on his way to becoming the most respected sword teacher in all of Japan. In our own times, on those infrequent occasions when a sword's sharpness and durability are to be tested, the sword is tested against bundles of matting or bamboo or wrapped straw. But in the ancient days in Japan, swords were tested against a much more demanding target—human bodies.

Gruesome as this practice may seem now, test cutting on bodies was an esteemed art during Japan's feudal era. It was carried out according to strict procedures, and on the tang of many a *katana* is inscribed the successful results of the tests. Bodies (usually those of condemned criminals) were held suspended by ropes or stacked on a packed sand platform. Various test cuts were made and rated according to a scale of difficulty. A clean blow through the pelvis was very hard to execute correctly; while severing a wrist the same way was not considered much of a feat. Test cutting, or *tameshigiri* as it is called in Japanese, was such an important skill that a couple of families specialized in it, founding schools and teaching their specific techniques. Yamada Sadatake was a student of the headmaster of the oldest school devoted to tameshigiri, the Yamano ryu. He inherited his master's abilities and earned a reputation for himself that brought him steady employment from some of Japan's best sword smiths, including the smith who supplied weapons for the shogun.

Tameshigiri is not an easy art. Human bones are tough and resilient, and unless a strike is coordinated perfectly, with the proper alignment between the tester's body, his grip, and his sword, mistakes can easily occur. Blades swung by testers were often masterpieces. A stroke that was just a hair off could damage a weapon irreparably. It happened. It happened if a small wooden plug holding the blade in the socket of the handle was not tight or if the blade was improperly seated in the handle. It happened to one tester, Matsushige Asasuka, one morning as he attempted to make a cut called a *tai-tai* to test an enormously valuable sword of the Bizen style, forged by Nobumitsu, as Yamada and a group of smiths looked on. Matsushige's aim was to cut the body before him in half, just below the rib cage. But his swing missed the correct path by just a fraction, and the sword hit the corpse's spine at an awkward angle. There was a sickening *chunk*. Matsushige paled. When he withdrew the blade and wiped it clean, everyone saw the nick in the edge.

There was no question in Matsushige's mind as to what he should do to rectify the situation. Two days later he committed suicide as a way of apologizing for his error. But the incident left Yamada with doubts and a sudden uncertainty about his own skills. "That could easily have been me instead of Matsushige," he told himself. "With all my experience, I am still dependent on little more than luck."

A sword tester was not all that different in his mental attitude toward his craft from a diamond cutter. The mediums are different, true. Yet the sword tester, like the diamond cutter, had to deliberate and concentrate, and his fortunes, like those of the diamond cutter, depended on a single blow. Also like a diamond cutter, whose nerves may suddenly shatter from the pressure of the occupation, Yamada found himself breaking out into a cold sweat at the very thought of picking up another katana. He sat up far into the night, reflecting on past tests he'd done, worrying about those he would have to do sometime soon. For days he agonized until finally he sought out a Buddhist priest. When he explained the problem, the priest had an odd solution: "Go see Oeda-sensei," the priest told Yamada.

"Oeda-sensei?" Yamada exclaimed. "But he is a teacher of *ikebana,* a man who arranges flowers for a living!" It was true. Oeda-san was a master of the Ikenobo style of flower arranging, a school of the art that specialized in *rikka,* the huge arrays of plants and blossoms that were used in temples to decorate the altars. What ikebana had to do with the art of tameshigiri, Yamada hadn't the slightest idea. He did not get a clue when he first visited Oeda-sensei's home, either. The flower master merely nodded when Yamada showed him the letter of introduction the priest had written. When Yamada explained his anxieties and their cause, Oeda sent him to watch some of the junior assistants who were bending pine branches that were to be used as part of a large rikka-style composition.

Branches for arrangements in the rikka mode must be gripped and bent slightly to form the shape the arranger has in mind. Bending a branch or a stem too weakly won't do any good; it will just straighten right back out. Too much pressure, though, and the stiffer branches and stems will break. Bending pine branches requires just the right touch, as Yamada learned when, after a week of observing the assistants, he was finally allowed to give it a try himself. *Crack!* The branches, all three that he had been given to bend, broke under the pressure of his grip.

"When you bend the branch, you have only one chance," one of the assistants told him. "Put all of yourself into the moment. One encounter with the branch, one chance to make it bend as you wish and be turned into an object of beauty." And with this bit of instruction, Yamada reached an enlightenment of sorts. He understood that like the practitioner of the Ikenobo style of flower arranging, he had no use for thoughts of past or future efforts in his practice of tameshigiri. Only absolute concentration on the present, on the moment at hand, could ensure a flawless execution of the strokes that were required of his profession. And with this insight Yamada Sadatake returned to his craft, and we are led to believe that never again did he hesitate, nor did he ever damage any of the blades that he tested.

Last spring I attended a lecture and a demonstration of the Ikenobo school of flower arranging by a highly ranked sensei. I was introduced to him before the event began, and we spent a few moments chatting. He had relatives near where my sensei in Japan lived, so he discovered that I had a background in the martial arts and Ways. While he was composing a huge display of rikka, he spoke of *ichi-go, ichi-e,* one encounter, one chance. He explained that this was a concept common to flower arranging and to the Way of the sword. While others in the audience may have been thinking of compositions of daffodils and iris, I was reminded of Yamada Asayemon Sadatake, the sword tester.

Note: Obviously, I have embellished this tale of Yamada with some details that I hope make it more readable. But he was a real person, he was one of the most famous sword testers of his day, and the events that led to his mental crisis and the solution he found in the art of flower arranging actually happened.

Chapter Seventeen

A Straight Shadow

Katachi tadashi kereba kage naoshi. (If the form is straight, the shadow will be straight.)

The phone call was from one of my editors who wanted a few autobiographical paragraphs about me for the back of a book I had written about the martial Ways. So I sat down and wrote a couple that I thought would fill the bill.

I listed the names of my various sensei, the teachers who had taught me, and their teachers, and their teachers. I listed the classical martial ryu with which I was affiliated. I made brief mention of a few of the exponents of those ryu who had descended from the same lineages I had, along with some of their accomplishments. One had fought—on the winning side, fortunately—during the battle of Sekigahara in 1600. Another had participated in a famous siege. Another had once given instruction in both swordsmanship and the tea ceremony to a member of the family of the sixth Tokugawa shogun.

All this information is contained in what is known in Japanese as a *keizu*—a genealogy of sorts, or a pedigree. Any serious exponent of a classical martial art can rattle off his lineage until long after the average listener is tired of hearing it. A keizu often begins so far back that the first names in it are semilegendary, in fact. I skipped a lot of that in the paragraphs the editor asked me to write, in the interest of saving space. Still I hoped he would be pleased with the information I did include.

He wasn't. He called me when he received my keizu. "I wanted you to tell me about yourself," he said. "You just told me about where you came from in the martial arts, not about who you are."

I did not have to think very long about my reply. "Where I came from *is* who I am."

The importance of lineage in martial arts can be a difficult concept for many Westerners and even for a lot of modern Japanese. When asked to tell something about himself, many Occidental budoka will typically respond with, "Well, I am a black belt such-and-such degree, I've won this tournament," and so on. This kind of person perceives himself largely in terms of his own accomplishments. Reading through magazines and many books devoted to the martial Ways, you will find story after story about renowned tournament champions or popular teachers, with not a single mention on their part of who trained them and taught them. Indeed, it is rare to find among these kinds of practitioners even one who can name his own teacher's teacher.

Such an attitude may speak to the American's singular sense of identity. One of the wonderful advantages the United States has always offered has been the chance to become your own person, independent of who your ancestors were. We are the country that created the "self-made man." Or, more accurately, the United States allowed him the freedom to create himself. Yet in terms of the budo, identifying ourselves based on our own accomplishments must be tempered with an awareness of our own past. As it is with great wines, within the structure of the traditional martial Ways, merit is determined, to some degree at least, by one's provenance, by the quality of one's keizu.

The reasons for this are varied. First, those who have followed the Japanese arts and Ways have done things this way for centuries. Knowledge of family background was crucial during the feudal era when out of the warrior class of old Japan there emerged some of the most famous family names in the history of that country. (By tradition and law, for instance, the Imperial line was continued through only a handful of families. Many other privileges and powers depended upon the hereditary status of the family group.) It is no coincidence that many of these same names appear in the early dojo roll books of judo, aikido, and kendo schools. The leaders of these budo forms knew that the presence of members with noble samurai ancestry would help establish the reputation of their dojo. (Of course, just because a man's family was famous or aristocratic did not guarantee that he was a worthy person. There were some extremely sleazy people in the prewar dojo of aikido's Morihei Uyeshiba and judo's Jigoro Kano, even though these people's backgrounds were what we would call in the West "blue blood.")

Secondly, we are speaking of disciplines in which ability can be conclusively demonstrated only by lethal ends. If you tell me that you are a fifth degree black belt in some system of karate, I still don't have much of an idea of how hard you can punch. But if you tell me that your teacher was so-and-so and his teacher was so-and-so, and I recognize those names, if I know them to be teachers of high quality and excellent reputations, then I have at least some indication that you may be a reasonably good practitioner as well. Who one is can be more safely and civilly ascertained by an explanation of his background rather than by a request for a demonstration.

Finally, though, and most important, I believe, the reason our historical pasts are so vital in our budo practice has little to do with establishing a reputation or with proving our abilities. It has very little to do with anyone else at all, in fact. Instead, the true value of understanding and relating to our own past is that it imparts a real sense of who we are. Knowledge and respect for our past gives us a rare kind of self-awareness. I have a feeling this is why so many people in our society are now busily engaged in looking for their roots, in studying the genealogy of their family, digging through old documents and census records, trying to find out who great-great-aunt Sally married or where an ancestor fought during the Civil War. In a society that has for so long looked to the future for its sense of well-being, growing numbers of people now appear to be searching the past to help them understand their world and, by extension, to help them understand themselves.

The martial Ways are no different. Since they were introduced to the West, the emphasis has been on improving and advancing them. Changes have come about in the performance of the kata and other techniques, and some practitioners have suggested that a whole new form of the budo is emerging, one geared entirely to Western sensibilities. Perhaps. But I notice more and more budoka are dissatisfied with this evolution. They seem to feel they have traded a priceless knowledge and comprehension of the past for a shallow and eventually pointless kind of future, and they have stopped moving in that direction in their own training. They have begun to look back, into the origins of their own budo forms, and into the older classical systems of combat in Japan that predate these Ways. They have begun to look as well into the related history and culture of old Japan that gave shape to the budo in the first place.

These budoka are sensing, I suppose, that the correctness and integrity of their art and the art as it was practiced and studied by those who came before them can play a big part in shaping their own character. That is what keizu is all about. It gives us a form, a structure. And just as we are influenced by it, we, who are in its shadow, will embody the solidity and soundness of the genealogy that is always behind us.

Chapter Eighteen

Count to One Hundred

Recently I was reading an article on the basics of wilderness survival. I don't spend all that much time in the deep wilderness, but I am a chronic worrier. I can always imagine that the airplane I'm on is going to crash on some mountain or my car is going to drive off a cliff way out in the woods and I'll have to survive on my own. So I habitually read wilderness survival articles when I run across them, hoping to pick up some tidbit of information that will teach me to make a solar heater out of my shoelaces or something. Anyway, when lost, stranded, or faced with a survival situation, this particular article I was reading noted that it is a good idea to pause long enough to count to one hundred. This advice seems pretty sound to me. The time it takes to count that far allows your mind to relax enough to absorb the situation objectively and to focus your concentration on the task at hand, which is surviving. A few moments spent occupying the consciousness with a simple, repetitive job can be very beneficial. This is, not coincidentally, a central goal of the *Do,* the Japanese Ways such as the tea ceremony and calligraphy. When the visitor to the tea hut pauses outside to rinse his mouth and hands from the water basin that is always there, it is a moment for him to clear his mind of the distractions of the regular world. When the calligrapher sits down and rubs an ink stick against the stone well, mixing it with water, he is preparing his medium, but he is also doing the same thing, calming his thoughts, centering his mind.

We count to one hundred in the martial Ways as well, although too few practitioners take advantage of the natural opportunties they have to do so while training at the dojo. And while survival may have a different meaning in the training hall than it does in the wilderness, the time you take to prepare yourself for the rigors of budo practice can be vital. This moment comes frequently during training, yet it is not a special event. It comes at the very ordinary interval when the practitioner pauses to bow.

It is common—and quite correct—to assume that *tachirei* and *zarei* (standing and sitting bows) are courtesies to be observed while practicing the budo. It is incorrect, though, to believe that these movements are nothing more than courtesies. Consider as an example the opening of a karate class. In most cases the students line up, assume a seated position, then bow to the dojo shrine, the teacher, and to their seniors, all in a preset manner that rarely varies from class to class. As the ritual unfolds, the minds of the practitioners are brought into a state of refined concentration; matters outside the dojo are temporarily put on hold. What is important is the lesson, the training, the direct experience of facing yourself through attacks and defenses against others.

Karate-do, like all the budo forms, can be remarkably dangerous. A single error by either participant is likely to result in some injury. As the skill of the karateka increases, the potential threat of inflicting or sustaining damage increases with it. At the beginner's level of *yakusoku kumite* (prearranged exchanges of technique), for instance, both the attack and the counters are usually weak and poorly focused. There is too much for the beginner to remember; he's concentrating on technical details, and at any rate, he lacks, the ability and coordination to make a strong action either offensively or defensively. A mistake by either partner at this level of training may be painful, but it is unlikely to be much more than that. Yet as time goes by the karateka learns to make stronger attacks. The consequences of a mistake become more serious. The advanced karateka must more and more try to enter into his regular practice with a complete grasp of the seriousness involved, of the real possibility of harming someone, or being hurt himself. For the exponent at this stage of training, the bowing and other such rituals of the dojo have a greater significance.

Within the older Japanese martial arts, those meant for actual use on the battlefield, the more advanced the training, the more intense the ritual that surrounds it. (More intense but not necessarily more elaborate, I must note. At a basic stage of training, there may be a protracted form of bowing and moving prefatory to actual practice, while at the more advanced levels the ritual may be simply a short bow. But there is an intensity to that bow that is much deeper and more concentrated than that which is found at the lower levels.)

Most modern budo like karate-do use only a couple of forms of bowing and a minimum of ritual prior to engaging in training. In the older arts, as I said, with their emphasis on battlefield effectiveness, the forms of ceremony are a necessity for getting into the heart of the matter. They may take some time to learn completely and to employ properly in teaching mental control and composure in the face of danger. In this kind of training, participants face one another before practice and may advance and retreat a set number of steps before or after bowing. They may bow, then place their weapons on the floor, backing away and bowing again before returning to take up the weapons and begin their exercise. The elaborate nature of this kind of *reishiki* (etiquette) surrounding these classical arts suggests that these rituals are not merely quaint anachronisms as nonpractitioners may suspect. They are, instead, a dynamic method for preparing the exponent mentally and spiritually for the rigors that are to follow. They are a way of counting to one hundred. Although the modern budoka might not ever experience these arts and rituals and this kind of training, he should try to adopt a similar serious and focused attitude when preparing for his own practice.

The obvious question is, what about those fighting arts and schools in which the bow is a quick nod and a slap of thighs with the hands? Well, as I mentioned earlier, the more serious the art, the more important the ritual. If the martial arts practitioner is content to confine himself to the limited endeavors of sparring and dance routines—which are so often all that is to be learned at certain schools and under certain systems—he has no need of any real kind of ritual. If he wishes to devote himself to a serious budo, which demands confronting the essential matters of life and death, then it seems inevitable that the mental preparations he will need to make in his training will be as studied and intense as those required for surviving in mortal combat.

Chapter Nineteen

Time

The cathedral at Chartres in France took over one hundred years to build. A century. That means that the stonemasons who laid the foundations for the cathedral there did so knowing that they would probably not be alive to see their work finished. The architects who designed and supervised the Chartres cathedral worked from plans on paper and in their minds that would not be realized in stone and mortar until long after they were dead and forgotten. These are facts I like to keep in mind when I have to stand a whole three minutes in McLine, waiting for my cheeseburger.

The difference between me and the builders of the Chartres cathedral is an enormous one, measured not just in terms of the time that has elapsed between the age in which they lived and the one in which I am now alive, but also by our vastly disparate *concepts* of time.

Prior to the modern era, man had a view of time that was measured far differently than it is today. Consider, for instance, the time it would take you to get a loaf of freshly baked bread if you decided this afternoon to have some with your dinner tonight. Likely, it is a matter of minutes to the nearest bakery where you can buy a loaf of bread that came from mechanically reaped and processed grain, machine milling, automated mixing, kneading, baking, and packaging. Yet for our ancestors, as little as a mere century ago, each of those processes had to be done by hand. When I say, "I need some bread," I am indeed talking about the same foodstuff our forefathers ate, more or less. But that is about the only thing that my statement has in common with what those before us meant when they uttered the same sentence.

Modern man usually tends to think in terms of hours when he talks of segments of time. Listen for it in the conversations around you. We work, most of us, a forty-hour week. Automobile—even jet travel—is measured in the hours it takes to go from one place to another. Not coincidentally, our education is calibrated in terms of so many credit hours or subjects studied. The generations before us, however, thought of time in different terms. Travel could take days or weeks, and long-distance ocean travel by ship could take months or even years. My great-grandfather worked aboard whaling ships that went off on voyages lasting two years or more. Education then was largely of the apprenticeship variety, and rather than classes lasting so many hours a student might spend years learning his craft. The students of Rembrandt, for example, were required to spend up to three years just learning to grind pigments for the paint that was used in the painter's studio.

It is tempting to conclude that one way of looking at time is better than another, that the "old, slow way" is inherently better than the "instant" way we are accustomed to now, or vice versa. But that is an oversimplification. The fact is, each generation tends to find what works best for it and for the particular circumstances of life that generation experiences. The problem occurs when we attempt to apply our concept of time to things of another age. Builders put up prefabricated churches today in a matter of weeks. That's okay. What is *not* okay is for contractors to try to convince the parishioners that their new church is as good, as well-built, as the Chartres cathedral. Art students graduate with a few hours of instruction and somehow believe they are on an artistic level with the masters of old. And martial artists think, some of them anyway, that in a matter of hours they can grasp the skills of arts that actually take more than a lifetime to really understand.

One of the favorite catchphrases heard in some martial arts circles is "absorb what is useful." The advice behind the phrase is to study a variety of combative arts and to distill from each of them what is worthwhile or applicable to you. It is a notion that is thought to be revolutionary and totally in opposition to the way "traditional" martial artists have always done things— sticking with a single art or school for the entirety of their training. But actually the notion of absorbing knowledge from different disciplines has strong roots in the budo and even in the *bujutsu* arts of the samurai that preceded them. The late Takaji Shimizu, the last headmaster of the Shindo Muso ryu of *jodo*, the art of the stick used against a sword, urged members of his ryu to take the "absorb what is useful" route. After they had completed the curriculum of the Shindo Muso ryu, he advised them to go out and learn from others. And he encouraged his students to integrate what they learned elsewhere into their jodo practice. But there is a crucial difference between what Shimizu-sensei was advising his students to do and the smorgasbord-type approach to the combative arts that is being advocated by some martial arts teachers today. The latter seem to be proposing that students study a martial Way for a few months or a few years and then extract its best features. Shimizu's Shindo Muso ryu cannot be learned—you cannot even be exposed to all of the kata in it—in less than ten years. It takes at least twice that long to get a good grasp of the essence of the ryu and to be able to see exactly what it is that is worth absorbing. The traditional martial arts and Ways, you see, are not modern creations. They operate on a different scale of time.

Are you a karateka who wants to add the techniques of aikido to your arsenal? Fine. Head on down to the aikido dojo. And after you have spent a decade or so training, you will be in a position to start absorbing what is useful from aikido. Until then, though, you are just learning. You are being exposed to the techniques and to the fundamentals behind them. You have no basis upon which to decide what is useful and what isn't, any more than a couple of cooking lessons learning to make a beef stock would enable you to make informed decisions about what is necessary or superfluous in French cuisine.

This advice, to go out and spend ten years or more studying something simply so you can extract from it some useful elements, may seem excessive. If so, it is probably because you are applying modern time frames to things that are not modern. Would you expect to paint like a fifteenth-century Flemish master by attending a semester of an art class? Could you reasonably hope to tap into even the most basic of his secrets of preparing a canvas, blending paints, applying finishes? And these are only minor technical details, mind you. We are not even considering the acquisition of the master's genius for composition, lighting, and so on. Only the most boorish among us would be so presumptuous as to think we could match the master's art without decades of special training. Well, martial arts are just that: arts. Their basics and secrets and subtleties are no less complex than those of the fine arts. Yet for some reason, individuals often approach them as if they could be completely understood and appreciated in a few hours.

This advice may strike the practitioner as discouraging. We are, after all, a product of our age. Ours is an era characterized by high speed, the instant, the attitude "I want it now." Quite often the prospective budoka's first step in beginning his training must be toward restructuring his sense of time. Instead of being put off because the demands imposed by the budo involve years rather than hours, the student should approach this learning as a new and different experience. Instead of expecting the arts to conform to his sense of time and then working to distort, pervert, and dilute them until they do, he should strive to adapt himself to the constructs of the budo, try to meet them on *their* unique terms, not try to force them to fit his own. When he makes this accommodation, the budoka is apt to discover what those who have gone before him have learned, too—the same thing I'll bet those builders of the Chartres cathedral knew as well. Whether one is building a cathedral or mastering a martial Way, when something is worth doing, and worth doing well, time is not important.

Chapter Twenty

Tsune ("Daily Habits")

The fortunate person learns that true happiness in life can be achieved only though constant dedication to disciplined habit in daily living. Only when a person is able to willingly undertake a pattern of living in which he deprives himself of all excesses can he find a content and balanced life, and his function on earth be said to be fulfilled.

—Koun Suhara

Koun Suhara is a senior priest at the Engakuji, the Zen Buddhist temple in Kamakura Japan, where, incidentally, the spirit of karate's Gichin Funakoshi is enshrined. In addition to his duties as a priest of the temple, Suhara is an enthusiastic practitioner of *kyudo* (Japanese archery) and *iaido* (sword drawing). His words on daily living describe eloquently the concept of what is called in Japanese *tsune,* or training as a matter of "everyday habit."

"Tsune" is a word usually applied to such activities as brushing one's teeth or attending to other such routine tasks that we all do from one day to the next without giving them much thought. In terms of the budo, tsune refers a the level of experience and involvement in which the training process becomes so integrated into one's lifestyle that it is a part of the daily routine. When the budoka reaches a point where he practices his Way as a tsune, it is almost certain that the art has "stuck" with him, that he will continue on the path of the budo for the rest of his life.

Prior to reaching what could be called the "tsune stage" of his training, the budoka undergoes a struggle. Not only is he dealing with the acquisition of the technical skills of whatever budo form he is pursuing; he is also fighting to make the practice fit into the fabric of his life. This is not as easy as it may sound. When he begins his practice, the new budoka's enthusiasm is almost always high and his motivations for going to class or training regularly are strong. The learning curve for a typical practitioner starts with a brief, slow period. There are endless details to learn, from bowing to the basics of stance and simple footwork. The lessons can be intimidating, but the enthusiasm of the beginner almost always takes him through this relatively tough stage without problem. Once the student has been introduced to the basics, the learning curve typically shoots up steeply. Every practice session is a new experience, some new technique added, some new insights gained. The budoka can't wait for the next class. This period of rapid learning can last for quite a while. Sooner or later, though, there is a leveling-off stage. The sensei is offering fewer new techniques. Instead the budoka is expected to begin to polish what he's already been taught. Furthermore, he has now become so comfortable in the dojo that he has the chance to look around and see some of the senior practitioners and even some of the practitioners at his own level. They may seem to be doing the movements and the methods so much better than he is, with so little effort. He has an opportunity to compare himself with others, and when he does there is likely to be some frustration and disappointment.

Furthermore, at the same time that the practitioner's progress slows, the initial novelty of the budo will start to wear off. What began as an exciting and challenging change in his routine has now become, well, routine. The budo, any of them, take a lot of time. They can interfere with personal relationships, hobbies, and other forms of relaxation. So when he is not learning quite so quickly, not learning quite so much, he may be tempted to skip a session here and there. There is an endless parade of excuses for *not* going to the dojo. "I've got a cold coming on." "I have a lot of work to do tonight." "I really deserve a rest. Maybe I'll get back to practice after the holidays." These thoughts arise like bubbles in a pot of boiling water when it comes time to go to the training hall. Sometimes the trainee makes escuses because he is lazy and was never really motivated to follow the budo in the first place. But other times the would-be budoka is perfectly serious about his commitment, yet it still seems there is always this or that engagement coming up in his life that gets in the way of his regular practice.

In a way, this period of the budoka's training is a test, one that every serious student will face. Not all will pass it. Some will find that their lives are organized in such a way that they are never able to accommodate regular training in a martial Way. For those who persevere, though, there is, after a time, the realization that tsune has begun to work its way into their training and so into their lives. It happens gradually. Without his realizing it, the budo the student has chosen to follow has become a part of his routine. He no longer thinks about it, no more than he would sit around and contemplate the process of making his bed in the morning or taking out the trash. In fact, if circumstances require him to miss class, he may feel as though something is missing in his life, as if he went to bed without taking off his clothes first, or neglected to comb his hair before he went out the door in the morning. He has, at this point, woven his particular martial Way into the fabric of his life. It will remain there for him, a tsune of his life.

Chapter Twenty-one

Strategy for the Modern-Day Battlefield

The story of Kamiizumi Nobutsuna and the rice balls has been repeated so many times that surely every reader knows it. It was even worked into the plot of the classic movie *The Seven Samurai.* Nobutsuna, a famous sixteenth-century swordsman who founded the Shinkage ryu of martial arts, was traveling in Owari Province when he came across a commotion at the Myoko Temple. A crowd had gathered around a gardening shed beside the main temple. Inside, a deranged criminal had taken a child hostage. Threats, offers of supplication, even the tears of the child's parents had not worked with the madman. Nobutsuna surveyed the situation, then ordered a monk standing nearby to turn over his robe. Nobutsuna put the robe on, then had his head shaved to complete the disguise. He walked slowly up to the door of the shed, some balls of rice wrapped in seaweed in his hands.

"You must be hungry in there," Nobutsuna the "priest" said calmly. "How about something to eat?" With that, he rolled one of the rice balls toward the criminal, who, believing himself to be in no immediate danger from a priest, let go of the child long enough to reach for the food. And long enough for Nobutsuna to seize and subdue him, freeing the child.

It is, as I said, a well-worn tale. It is one that has been repeated almost as often as one about Tsukahara Bokuden and his "No Sword Method" of winning a fight. Bokuden, this legend goes, was aboard a ferry in Omi Province, sharing a ride across the lake with several other travelers. One of the men onboard was a particularly loud and belligerent samurai. He was extolling his martial skills and was evidently entertaining the fondest of hopes that one of the other passengers would challenge him to prove himself. When Bokuden reacted to all of these boasts by turning his back on the bully, the samurai approached him. "How about you," the samurai snapped at Bokuden. "You're wearing swords. What school are you from?"

"I practice the Mutekatsu ryu," Bokuden replied, meaning the "style of winning without a sword."

"What!" scoffed the bully samurai. "Absurd! I've never heard of such a ridiculous school."

This went on and on until Bokuden realized the bully would not be shut up and could not be talked out of fighting. He agreed to a match and suggested that the ferryman steer over to a sandbar where a suitable spot for a duel could be found. The ferryman complied. When the prow of the boat struck the sand, the samurai leaped out and began pacing up the slope to get to level ground. Bokuden took up an oar, and still standing in the boat he pushed it back into the lake. As the ferry slid away from the sandbar, stranding the bully, Bokuden shouted to him, "There you have it. An example of the techniques of the Mutekatsu ryu!"

When we read about the *heiho,* the principles of combative strategy that were employed by great warriors of old Japan, we are apt to think of these as only methods warriors used in life-threatening situations. Yet the strategies most often implemented by Japan's illustrious martial artists of the past were effective because they were applicable not just in the extremes of battle or duels, but also in daily life. For every duel or battle that men like Nobutsuna and Bokuden fought and won, they *avoided* ten others. They used their strategy far more often to avoid fighting than they did when actually fighting, and in no small way that is the secret of their martial success.

These men averted potentially dangerous encounters because they used a kind of planning and forethought that was peculiar to the life they led. A swordsman, for instance, would generally take care to position himself so his right hand was unencumbered; he needed to be able to draw his sword in an instant, and he didn't want to be caught holding a sack of apples in that hand when the time came to fight. Nor did he want to be standing in such a way that movement on his right side was blocked by, say, a doorway or a pillar. At night in a room he would habitually situate himself in such a way that any lamps in the room would be between him and the paper-screen walls. In that way, his silhouette would never present an easy, outlined target for an enemy outside. For the feudal warrior of old Japan, these were commonplace measures he took to equalize the risks of his rather special way of life. He dealt with potential dangers by using common sense. Although today we don't carry swords and don't worry constantly about the threat of assassins, using the same kind of common sense will often serve as a useful strategy in our lives.

All of this came to mind recently when I saw a young man leaving a dojo after a karate class, still wearing his *keikogi*, or training uniform. Anyone who wears a karate uniform or any kind of budo keikogi out on the street along with a pair of sneakers or hard-soled shoes looks a little silly. It is almost always a lower-ranked martial artist who does this; most of the more advanced budoka have learned that it is not at all appropriate to wear the clothes of the training hall outside, except on special occasions. Yet I have seen an aikido black belt show up for a demonstration and amble happily through a crowd of thousands wearing his keikogi and *hakama* skirt. He may have thought this made him look more "authentic," more serious or professional, and that he was establishing a presence for the demonstration he intended to give. But priests are serious, and they do not wear their vestments when they walk to church. Major league baseball players are professional, and they don't wear their uniforms to the stadium on game day.

There are practical reasons for not wearing a keikogi outside the dojo. Consider what your clean white uniform would look like after fixing a flat tire or crawling under the car to reattach a broken muffler. More important, though, wearing your keikogi out on the street is a good example of bad strategy.

Suppose you are driving home after martial arts training and your car runs out of gas, forcing you to make an unexpected hike to a gas station. I am sorry to say it, but the sight of a fellow walking down the road in a "kurroty suit" is almost certain to bring out the yahoo that is hidden not too far beneath the surface of some jerk passing by. The lout gives a derisive yell as he drives past you, and then he interprets your frightened jump as an invitation to fight. He slams on the brakes and jumps out to engage you. Suppose it goes beyond the level of a verbal taunt or two. Maybe he actually attacks you. You defend yourself, knock him down, and then the police arrive. "Arrest this guy," your attacker demands. "He threw a rock at my car and jumped me when I stopped." Of course, he might tell the same story about you and the incident even if you were wearing jeans and a T-shirt or slacks and a sport coat. But how much validity does his tale gain when he adds, "Look at him, he's a kurroty nut, walking around in that outfit looking for trouble"?

You see? You have unwittingly drawn yourself into a dangerous situation. And all because of bad strategy.

Wearing a keikogi on the way to or from the dojo may not seem like a big deal. Likewise, keeping himself in a position so as to be able to employ his sword instantly (or out of position so as not to be an easy target) might have seemed excessively paranoid or a waste of time to some samurai in the past. Most of the time, nothing would come of their preparation for trouble. Yet then again, it only takes once. Today's budoka need to consider this as well as other strategies that might help them avoid danger. If Bokuden were around today, would he be shopping at the local mall wearing a t-shirt that advertised his fencing school? Would Nobutsuna have a bumper sticker on his car advertising his martial style? Of course not. But come to think of it, if they did have t-shirts or bumper stickers, I suspect they might have liked one with this sentiment inscribed on it: STRATEGY. IT'S NOT JUST FOR THE BATTLEFIELD ANYMORE.

Chapter Twenty-two

Improve Yourself

"When the superior man fails to hit the target with his arrow," noted Confucius, "he looks for faults, not in his bow, but in himself."

More than one ethnologist has made the observation that when early Western archers in Europe ran up against limitations in their combative skills, they responded by improving their technology. They designed and fashioned better bows in response to any problems they encountered. When the Japanese archer encountered boundaries in his shooting abilities, he responded by improving himself. This comparison is a bit oversimplistic, admittedly. Still, it does acknowledge a fundamental distinction in the thinking of East and West, one that has had considerable influences on the budo and on the way in which they can sometimes be approached in dojo in the United States and in Japan.

A state-of-the-art bow in the West today is a weapon of space-age polymers or fiberglass or some other remarkable substance that is about as far removed from the wood used in bows in earlier times as titanium is from pig iron. The bow is equipped with pulleys, telescopic sights, string vibration suppressers—the bow a modern deer hunter uses in his sport would be scarcely recognizable to the Stone Age Indian of North America. Examine a Japanese bow or *yumi* that was made the day before yesterday, however, as compared with one that was made three centuries ago, and you will find not much difference at all. Both will have a core of laminations of sumac wood and bamboo, and both will have essentially the same shape. The dimensions of the yumi have been fixed in the art for many, many generations. There have been, in essence, almost no improvements to speak of in the technology of Japanese archery in several hundred years. So here we have two civilizations with two very different ways of approaching the same instrument.

Typical of his culture, the Westerner who has been introduced to the martial Ways of Japan can be reluctant to accept them uncritically. The idea that he should simply copy what his teachers are doing—never questioning, never contemplating possible improvements or changes that would benefit him—has probably never even occurred to him. Before they were long into their study of the budo, many Westerners were already busily making what they believed were modifications and additions to these Ways that would make them better. Weight training, scientifically examined stretching techniques before class and special cooldown exercises afterward, weight divisions for competitions—all of these are contributions to the budo scene made almost entirely by Western influences.

That we in the Occident have been discontented with the status quo, always eager to take chances and experiment with change, has been one of our greatest attributes and has made possible our many contributions to civilization. Still, our penchant or drive for what is technologically better has not been an unmixed blessing for us. Ignoring the wider stage of science and social changes and looking at those evolutions that Westerners have introduced to the budo, we can also see a downside to the constant demand for "improvements." Weight training, for instance, has doubtless improved the techniques and endurance of many budoka. Weight divisions in competition have just as certainly perverted the budo badly, grossly magnifying the importance of a silly sporting event in the minds of too many budoka and giving its results precedence over the real goals of the martial Ways. And warm-ups before training? Well, they're good in that they have prevented injuries. But they're bad in that they have encouraged an overemphasis on techniques like karate's head-high kicks and other such methods that are unnatural, unrealistic, and superfluous to mastering the physical principles of the art. So improvements are a mixed bag.

The real challenge of making what we think of as improvements in the budo is not in whether these changes are good or bad—they can be both and usually are. The heart of the matter comes in recognizing when such progress is important and needed and when it is merely a deviation from the Way. There comes a time, you see, when the budoka must realize the limitations of technology, when he understands and acts on the Confucian notion that he himself is to be responsible for his progress on this journey. If you are struggling with a kata or with a technique, you have several options. You can begin a weight-training program to make you stronger; you can read books on the kata or the method; you can watch videos that have been produced to explain things. It is a characteristic of our age that such resources are out there in profusion to assist—and to tempt—us. Yet in the end we must, like the Japanese archer, turn to ourselves if we are going to make progress. We must practice the kata or the technique, perfecting it as we struggle with the larger goal of the budo, which is, of course, to perfect ourselves.

To me the idea of working to perfect one's self is one of the most appealing and profound aspects of the budo. The martial Ways will allow those who pursue them all sorts of diversions along the path. There is nothing built into their structure that will keep you from going off on this or that tangent. Nevertheless, in the end, the path will be waiting, right where you left it, unchanged and still leading in the right direction. When the kata does not feel right, when the technique will not work, you can look to the assistance that might be provided by technology. Read a book, watch a video, take some exercise on the latest equipment. But sooner or later, know that you will have to look for the solution within yourself.

Chapter Twenty-three

Beauty and the Martial Way

Beauty in odd places, found in the most unexpected of realms...

When I was much younger, I began my practice of a form of classical Japanese martial art that involves training with at least a couple of weapons, including a long and a short sword. As with all of these classical arts, the bulk of my instruction and practice took place outside, in open fields and other such natural areas. While practicing the kata of the long sword, my teacher and I would place the short sword or *kodachi*, on the ground nearby. I noticed, after a while, that my sensei would spend a few moments looking around, searching for a special spot to put down his kodachi. Since we usually trained in a wide open field, there seemed to be little need to worry about exactly where to lay down the short sword, except to be sure it was far enough away to avoid our stepping on it during practice. So I was curious as to what it was Sensei was searching for as he looked around for the right spot. Finally, I began to watch more closely to see exactly what he was doing. Sensei did not do anything without reason, but if I came right out and asked him, he was unlikely to tell me what his reasons were. He preferred, I had learned by then, to teach by example, and it was part of my job as his student to figure out what was going on.

After watching him for a while, I realized that he always placed his weapon near something of beauty. Maybe it was a spray of little purple violets that bloomed early in the spring every year. It might be a bloom of dandelion in midsummer. In the fall, he would put the sword next to a colorful sycamore or oak leaf that had fallen and drifted. In the winter, it would be next to a tuft of hardy weeds that were brown and somberly elegant against the snow.

Many *kyudoka,* as practitioners of the Way of Japanese archery are called, will fix a blossom to the surface of the target just before they shoot at it.

Inserted under the braiding along the handle of the Japanese sword are small fixtures called *menuki.* Menuki serve, among other functions, as a form of friction to keep the silk braiding of the handle in place. The braiding, in turn, provides a good, nonslip purchase for gripping the handle. Any patterned piece of metal would suffice for this purpose, but menuki are miniature works of art. They are intricately designed, sometimes in abstract geometric forms; other times menuki depict animals or shapes found in nature such as seashells, flowers, or branches of foliage. I have one menuki in my modest collection that depicts a trio of fat and happy field mice scampering over a bale of straw. Another is a pair of rabbits playing beneath a crescent moon. There are enthusiasts all over the world who make it a hobby to collect menuki, tiny masterpieces that once felt the hands of the samurai on them, hot and sweaty in the exertions of life and death.

The modern budoka is apt to be parsimonious in acquiring new training equipment or uniforms. He will tend to use his wooden training weapons until they have become so brittle or splintered along their edges that they present a safety hazard, and by that time they will have acquired a beautiful patina created by perspiration, body oils, and the natural aging of the wood itself.

Although the traditional budoka today normally wears a white uniform, in the classical martial disciplines, the color of choice is almost always a deep indigo. There are some practical reasons for such a preference. Indigo tends to hide dirt and stains. In the colder months the dark color absorbs whatever heat the winter sun gives, not a small consideration when you are training outdoors in the cold. But certainly one reason for the prevalence of indigo as a color choice for training uniforms is that as it is worn and washed again and again, indigo fades and attains a wonderful, quiet beauty. This is the same kind of beauty to be found in the gently frayed and greying black belt that is worn around the waist of the advanced exponent of the modern budo forms.

Why is the martial artist attracted to things of beauty? What is it that makes him seek out beauty in the midst of his violent practice? These, I think, are fundamental questions for the serious budoka. He should look deeply into his training and his journey on the Way to see where beauty lies and to see, more important, what it means in the process of his own maturation as a martial artist.

Chapter Twenty-four

Climbing the Circular Ladder

The *shiai* (tournament) was over, and the five just-promoted black belts stood at erect attention before the seated board of tournament judges. All five had just received *batsugun,* or promotions granted by virtue of demonstrating skill in competition. Every one of them had been approaching the rank of black belt, but it was particularly dramatic that all of them had received batsugun at the same time. We lower-ranked *judoka* sat formally off to the lower side of the hall on the outer edge of the mats, awed. We hung on every word the tournament judges were saying, hoping that there would be some kernel of wisdom in their congratulatory speeches to the five, that the judges would say something that would be the key to our someday standing where those black belts were.

The last judge to speak was Nishimoto-sensei. Nishimoto was an *osho,* a Buddhist priest who oversaw the religious needs of parishioners, nearly all of the first-and second-generation Japanese Americans scattered all over Colorado and western Oklahoma. He was also a fifth-dan in judo, having trained at the Kodokan, the dojo in Tokyo that is headquarters for judo in Japan and all over the world. He worked as a judge at all our judo tournaments, and he also played a role in keeping us younger judoka in line and out of trouble. He had a way of imparting some rather pithy wisdom with a bare minimum of words, and he was not at all averse to using the back of his hand on our heads when a more immediate and forceful lesson was in order. When it was his turn to speak to the new black belts, Nishimoto stood, folded his arms across his chest, and addressed the five in front of him.

"You have taken a big step forward," he said, then he paused. "Now I hope you will take a big step back." Then he sat down.

It is typical and understandable that most of us tend to view all of our undertakings in a linear sense. That is, we think that our work, our learning, our relationships, everything we try to accomplish in life, will progress in a series of straight steps that go forward and upward the further along we go. We begin our public schooling in the first grade, then go on to the second, and so on. Military personnel "go up through the ranks." The company businessman works his way "up the corporate ladder." We all take things "step by step." Further, we all take it pretty much for granted that the progression to be sought is on a straight path. The second grader does not expect to have to go over the simple printing of the alphabet again. He already learned that in the previous grade and anticipates going on to something new. The recently promoted colonel in the army would be chagrined to say the least if he were sent out to practice close order drill again with some new recruits. The corporation vice president would not be at all thrilled to find himself learning simple secretarial chores. You get the idea.

And with that in mind, isn't it understandable that the third-dan black belt in judo might be just a little bewildered and angry at having to go back and polish the breakfall basics he learned the first time he practiced?

Kihon, or "basics," are the fundamentals of all the budo. They are the foundations upon which all other skills must be based. But nearly all martial artists look upon kihon as stepping stones, I think. The karateka learns the basics of assuming a strong stance so he can learn to make more balanced kicks, so he can then learn to make more powerful kicks, so he can learn to make spectacular *leaping* kicks against an opponent, and then against multiple attackers, and so forth. He sees the kihon as the first step in the process.

There is nothing wrong with this idea. Even the most dedicated among us would probably lose some of our enthusiasm for the budo if we thought we would never progress past mastering a basic stance or a simple, fundamental technique. But we would be seriously misleading ourselves if we came into our training with the notion that once a kihon is learned, we can go on and never give it another thought.

The martial Ways are an exception to the linear, step-by-step, vertical staircase concept of progress. It might be better to think of the budo as a circular or spiral staircase. Maybe the kind that goes up inside a lighthouse. Certainly both types of staircases go up, but you will bear in mind that the spiral staircase is an entirely different form of staircase than the straight-up kind. Peer over the railings of a spiral staircase at regular intervals and it will appear that you are not going anywhere. The fact is, of course, you are moving. You are going around and around. But you are, more to the point, always moving *up* as well. When the advanced kendoka comes to class and finds the lesson that night will be on the basic overhead strike to the forehead, he need not be disappointed at having to do *that* again. Not if he's smart. For returning to a lesson already learned is not like going back to the first grade. On the contrary, the kendoka understands that after practicing for some time he has progressed several flights up the staircase, compared to when he was first introduced to the strike. And although he is practicing the same technique as the beginner just learning it for the first time, the advanced kendoka is discovering all sorts of insights about the movement that are quite over the head of the beginner. Further, these insights are not a one-shot phenomenon. The kendoka will continue to learn new angles on the kihon regularly as long as he continues training. For weeks, maybe months, and later on for years, he will continue to practice, making the same strike over and over and then suddenly he will have the experience of "Hey, I never realized this before. That's what the secret of the overhead strike is."

What actually happens is that having made another revolution around the spiral staircase, the kendoka has undergone a change. The strike has not changed. His understanding and mastery of it have progressed. Another way of putting it would be as Nishimoto-sensei did in addressing those new black belts: Always be ready in your training to take a step back. After all, taking a step backward is the only way to get ahead in the budo.

Chapter Twenty-five

The Warrior and the Dirty Diaper

The dojo was rapidly filling with visitors who had come, some of them from several hundred miles away, for the aikido seminar. I was among those jostling for a space to take my shoes off out at the entrance. A young woman from Japan was next to me and bumped me as she was balancing on one foot, trying to pull her boot off the other. We introduced ourselves, and she asked if I'd been to this dojo before. I had, I told her, and so she asked me, "Do they have a restroom?"

"*Okawaya*," I said.

She laughed, then she corrected what she assumed was my outdated Japanese. "A more modern word for a 'restroom' is *o-tearai*," she informed me. "An okawaya means an 'outhouse.'"

I nodded. Then I led her back out the door into the bitter cold morning. I pointed to the bottom of the hill amidst a grove of bare oaks where one could just make out the silhouette of the dojo facilities.

"When I said *okawaya*," I replied, "I meant *okawaya*."

The rustic restroom was just one of the many enjoyments of this aikido dojo located out in the Ozarks countryside. It is a place that Morihei Uyeshiba, the founder of aikido, would have loved. He felt aikido practice went well with a lifestyle that included farming and rural living, and this dojo is miles from the nearest town, surrounded by forests and farmland. In the summer, there is a chorus of birds calling during evening practice, and the entire back wall of the dojo, which is a big, industrial-size garage door, can be opened. From this vantage point you look out on the woods and on the summer sunsets, which are so beautiful you are often distracted from your training by the view. In the winter, it's not unusual for deer to amble by, browsing on the grass outside the dojo and looking in to ponder the strange goings-on.

But the main reason so many of us were drawn to the countryside dojo that cold December weekend was to take advantage of the opportunity to learn from one of the seniormost non-Japanese aikido sensei in the United States. A fifth-dan with more than two decades of training in aikido and living in Japan, he was one of the most expert teachers many of those attending the seminar had ever practiced with. In addition to his expertise in budo, he was fluent in Japanese and had a degree in Japanese philosophy. His insights and comments about the martial Ways were invaluable. He called the class to order and lead us into what we all thought would be a short warm-up session. An hour later, we were still at it. The sensei showed us breakfall exercises that had even the advanced practitioners in the class stumbling awkwardly. After that, it was on to basics. The simplest movements of aikido he broke down and corrected and demonstrated for us. By the time we were beginning the fundamental techniques we are all perspiring, in spite of the cold that seeped in around the windows and door of the dojo.

The sensei motioned to me to come up and take falls for him as he demonstrated a throw he wanted us to work on. We bowed, stood, and I grabbed the wrist that he offered. Coming to grips with a teacher of such high skill is almost always a special experience. In aikido, it feels like an electric shock has seized your body. As I grabbed, he shifted, his body seeming to roll away from me, and suddenly I was airborne. To be thrown by someone of this level is like being caught in a force that envelopes and moves you at its own, irresistible will. The sensei was using but a fraction of his power as he led my attack away from him, mastering the swirl of energy, and I was tumbling through the air and then abruptly lying flat on the mat. I leaped up, grabbed again, and went through the same arc, landing on the other side of the mat. Back and forth he threw me, again and again, talking as he did, noting the aspects of the technique he thought we needed to work on. My body felt weightless, and it was almost as if he was cradling me, guiding me in my falls, keeping me under his control from the moment I began my attack until I was back on the mat again. Taking falls under such tutelage is often joyous, occasionally a bit frightening; it is always worthwhile, and sometimes it can be enlightening.

After the end of the day's training, the sensei went to the back of the dojo where his wife was sitting, watching their toddler at play on the corner of the mat. The sensei scooped the boy up—and caught a whiff of that aroma known all too well by all parents.

"You need a diaper change," he said. And that's what the sensei did. He found a place on the floor not occupied by students still practicing or talking. Still in his training uniform and hakama skirt, he put the boy down, took off the dirty diaper, and cleaned up a very messy bottom. He then outfitted his son in a clean, fresh diaper.

It was not a big gesture. Not nearly so dramatic as some of the spectacular throws he had shown us early in training. It was certainly not a display of awe-inspiring skill. Yet watching the sensei with his child, his gentleness, the matter-of-fact way he met the chores of fatherhood exactly as he had met the responsibilities of a senior teacher, I think I had a glimpse of what the martial Ways are all about. Strength and compassion. Power expressed through caring. The warrior as defined by his relationships with others, his love and deep humanity.

You can learn a lot in the long hours of a budo seminar. But every once in a while you can also get a bonus, in the oddest of ways. In the changing of a dirty diaper, for instance.

Chapter Twenty-six

What Kind of Shape Are Your Morals In?

I was once pressed into service as a translator for a karate sensei who was visiting a local dojo to conduct a training seminar. If there is such a thing as an ordinary karate sensei, this was not one of them. He was among the seniormost karate exponents of his generation, certainly the most expert I had ever met. One of the newspapers sent a reporter out to do a story on the teacher, and since the sensei's English was marginal, I was asked to translate when it was necessary. Sending a reporter with no background or understanding of the budo out to interview a budo teacher is like sending a book reviewer out to cover a tennis championship. The questions were, as I expected, rather shallow, most being along the lines of "How long did it take you to get a black belt?" and "Do you break boards in your practice?" That sort of thing. I was half-interestedly relaying the responses back and forth but at the same time I was also trying to give the reporter some idea of what a budo, a martial Way, was all about, and to explain just who this karate sensei was sitting there in front of him. To my surprise, the reporter seemed to pick up my message, at least a little bit.

"What does it take to be able to follow this 'Way' you're talking about?" he asked me, "What kind of qualities do you have to have?"

I translated the questions for the sensei, and he and I shared small, quick looks of shock that the reporter was pursuing such a reasonably intelligent line of inquiry. Then, without any further hesitation, the sensei replied, "Moral stamina."

At first I thought the sensei's answer was one of those odd neologisms that nonnative speakers will come up with. But the more I thought about it, the more appropriate his choice of words seemed to be. We don't often associate the idea of morals with stamina. We are more likely to equate stamina with some sort of physical activity. Most budoka are willing to undergo the challenges required of their bodies in pursuing the martial Way. The demanding practice sessions, the aching muscles and occasional injury—we accept these hardships as part of the overall package. The budo, however, involve much more than merely the development of physical skills or the perfection of technique. Morihei Uyeshiba's aikido, Jigoro Kano's judo, the karate of Gichin Funakoshi and others—the founders of each system of the modern budo made it clear that the development of character was a fundamental reason for the pursuit of these Ways.

Conventional thinking is that most practitioners of the various budo are drawn to martial arts initially for reasons of self-defense and self-confidence. This is probably true. I suspect, though, that many of us were attracted to the martial Ways because of the courage and integrity we saw embodied in many of their exponents. We saw these attributes in others who were traveling on the path of the budo, and we naturally hoped to develop them within ourselves. It was our intention, or at least one of our intentions, to polish and nurture these qualities, so we started along the martial path ourselves.

But noble ideals can come crashing down just as hard in the training hall as they can anywhere else in our lives and in our society. Maybe harder. For example, that invitation to the male senior for some "extra practice" time from the petite brown belt with the big blue eyes is a tempting one to accept—even if the senior practitioner is married. Her admiration for his skill is obvious, so why shouldn't he take advantage of the situation? And if it leads to a bit of a private dalliance between the two, well, who is hurt? It happens all the time in offices and elsewhere. Or how about the third-dan's gripe about the martial arts organization he's belonged to for years? So many times it has charged outrageous rates for testing, promoted others around him purely for the political gain of the organization, cheated and disappointed him so many times, so finally he resigns. But the leaders were getting ready to promote him to fourth-dan; that was obvious. So why not just go ahead and claim the rank that was going to be his anyway in a matter of months? Then there are those long-term, keep-paying-even-if-you-quit contracts you, as a teacher, require your students to sign—purely for their own good, of course, you tell yourself. Perhaps you have an urge to show off a bit in training, or to slack off a little. In whatever form the misbehavior comes, the ideals with which we began treading the martial Way are slowly, sometimes almost imperceptibly, eroded each time we put the desire for prestige ahead of our principles or each time we give in to our greed, our lust, or our laziness.

It is at such moments that the stamina of our morals is tested. Have we the endurance to stay the course on which we started? Or, once off it, have we the inner resources necessary to get up, brush ourselves off, and start back again on the right path?

It would be nice to say that a lot of us *do* have the ability to recover from such mistakes or to see them coming and avoid them in the first place. But the sad truth is that a lot of us do not. The martial Way is long and steep at times; it is not always very well lit or simple to follow. And it is devilishly easy to convince yourself that you are still going in the correct and true direction when you are, in fact, headed the opposite way. It is all too simple, in all aspects of life but particularly in the budo, to convince yourself that you are moving forward when in actuality you have stopped and are no longer serving as a model to others on the journey; instead you are merely another obstacle for them to get around. The only way to avoid losing your way is to maintain a healthy sense of morality. Without this anchor, no matter how strong, how talented, or even how dedicated you are to mastering the budo, you haven't a chance of reaching your goal.

And so, as the karate sensei noted when asked just what it takes to follow the martial Way, just as you should assess your physical fitness from time to time, so, too, it is a good idea to occasionally stop and think about what kind of shape your morals are in.

Chapter Twenty-seven

Martial Artist or Martial Artisan?

Those of us who follow the paths of karate-do, judo, kendo, aikido, or some other Japanese martial discipline use the term "martial artist" when describing ourselves. I use it as well in speaking and in writing. If I actually think about it, I tend to think of myself, as a martial *artisan*. I have felt that way ever since reading, years ago, something the potter Shoji Hamada said.

The late Shoji Hamada, whose life spanned the first three quarters of the twentieth century, was one of the outstanding figures of modern Japanese art. In the years before World War II, Hamada, a potter by trade, launched an investigation into the profound traditions of Japanese pottery as produced by the common people of that country for centuries. Along with Soetsu Yanagi, Hamada eventually influenced pottery technique and design throughout the world, and Hamada is primarily responsible for the revival of *mingei,* the folk art of Japan. It may seem that an artisan, involved with a delicate art like pottery would have little of relevance to say about an activity as rigorous as the budo. But I think that some of Hamada's comments speak eloquently of the spirit that energizes all of those who take an interest in things traditional, whether that interest takes the direction of art that is folk, fine, or, in our case, martial. I believe, too, that what he said on the subject of artists and artisans reflects on the struggle faced by the budoka who is intent on creating for himself a true Way of life in the martial path that he walks along daily.

"There are two kinds of people," said Hamada, "those who make themselves the center, who live as though their ancestors lived only to create them; and those who make themselves as low as possible, consider themselves nothing in relation to the whole, live in order to protect and cherish what their ancestors lived for and who bear children in order to pass on that idea of protecting and cherishing. Most artists fall into the first classification. Most artisans are in the second one."

Can you think of any description that more perfectly delineates what it is that separates the serious budoka from the one who enters the martial Ways merely to satisfy his own ego or for other similarly self-centered reasons?

I am always amazed at those individuals who speak and behave as if the whole of the martial Ways were devised and refined for no other reason than to benefit them. One sees this attitude quite commonly among the so-called "martial arts actors," and other such types who seem to receive so much attention these days. Accolades have been heaped on them for all they have supposedly done to promote the budo through the movies and public appearances. Of course, they have really done just the opposite. They have used the budo to promote themselves. Not long ago I read an autobiography of one of these actors who has starred in a string of silly and violent movies and his own series on television. The book ran slightly more than one hundred pages, yet he devoted less than one page to mention of his martial arts teacher. In the world of karate tournament champions and "masters" who constantly vie for attention through the media, the same mentality is often in evidence. These people rarely acknowledge even having had a teacher, never mind crediting their teachers with some of their success.

These examples of egocentrics are in marked contrast to the attitude of the "artisan" type that Hamada described so well. The artisan, if he is a potter like Hamada, sees little reason to sign his work, for instance, or to otherwise draw attention to himself. If he is a budoka, he places little value on displaying his trophies or in adorning himself with glitzy costumes or extravagant titles like "Grand Master." All artisans avoid affectations like these not because of false modesty, but because they recognize that their role in the greater scheme of these arts and Ways—no matter what they may accomplish—is very minor. The artisan is like the high school journalism student who after his first article appears in the school paper resists calling himself an "author." He does not give in to the temptation to glorify his accomplishment because he is keenly aware that the library down the hall is filled with the works of writers like Tolstoy, Melville, and Dryden. In other words, without failing to take pleasure in his accomplishment, he sees it in the greater context of the world's writers and knows that a sense of proportion is necessary to have a healthy understanding of what it is he has done.

Artists, to use Hamada's analogy, perceive themselves as the pinnacle, the top of whatever pyramid—writing, painting, martial art—they have chosen to ascend. They may not believe they are the best or the most talented or the most successful, but they do see their medium primarily as a means by which to express themselves. Artisans, on the other hand, regard themselves more as links in a chain, as part of a tradition, and their primary aim is to continue that tradition. The weakness of a pyramid's top block is that from such an elevated position it is impossible to see the rest of the structure that supports you. (Art majors in most colleges and universities have only a rudimentary knowledge of art history and the artists who have preceded them, just as most competition-minded martial artists haven't much comprehension of the evolution and significant figures in the past in their disciplines.) That doesn't happen when one is part of a chain. A chain link is in constant contact with the links behind it. The person who is a link in a chain is aware of the support that precedes him. And he tends to be a stronger individual for it.

Another weakness for the one who is on top of a pyramid is that it is a position, a narrow point, from which little else can be built. There is no balance there. The tip of the pyramid is after all the final part of the structure's construction. A chain, on the other hand, is perfect for making additions, since an infinite number of links can be added, as long as each is as strong as those behind it, so that each link can be added without doing any harm to the structure.

There may be budoka out there who are truly artists in the sense that they are men or women so creative, so brilliant and utterly original that they are capable of devising worthwhile new forms of the budo, providing a work of art that expresses some function never before addressed in the martial Ways. I am quite completely confident that I am not among them. For me, to be an artisan in the budo is a tough enough task. I may not make it to the top of anything, and it's more likely I will be just another anonymous link in the chains of those budo I have elected to follow. But considering that as an artisan I will be in the company of links the likes of Shoji Hamada, that is a chain on which I can comfortably live.

Chapter Twenty-eight

Simple Things

Victory and defeat are determined by attention to simple things.

—Gichin Funakoshi

Although this is one of the twenty maxims for training and daily life that Gichin Funakoshi left specifically for his own karate students in the Japan Karate Association, it has as much meaning today for budoka of all persuasions as it did for Funakoshi's pupils. Maybe more.

As most students of Japanese arts or Ways will know, for nearly all elements of Japanese culture there are facets which are *omote* and those which are *ura*. The omote is that which is on the "outside," which is obvious and discernible at first glance. The ura, or "reverse," is hidden and often requires some digging, some persistence, some special insight and sensitivity to grasp. Funakoshi's maxim is also subject to interpretation in terms of omote and ura. The outer meaning of the karate master's words is some very practical advice about practicing the martial Way, specifically about *kihon*, or basics. Kihon are the foundation of any budo. If they are not strong, thoroughly welded and interconnected, you can forget about building anything substantial and long lasting atop them.

Once you have carefully and painstakingly laid the foundation of the kihon, however, you cannot simply forget about them. Basements leak if they are not periodically waterproofed. You have to go down and check the beams from time to time if you want to be sure that the house above remains safe and stable. These are simple matters in maintaining a house. In the dojo, such simple matters are found in working on the kihon.

It is possible to distinguish beginners from experts in the training hall by watching them warm up prior to a practice session. The beginners will be fine-tuning the last technique or skill they have learned; the experts will likely be going over the first fundamentals they were taught, the kihon.

The following story, one cherished and repeated over and over by those who knew Shimizu-sensei, illustrates this point. Takaji Shimizu, the last headmaster of the Shindo Muso ryu of *jodo* (the art of the stick as it is employed against a sword) introduced his art to many Westerners living and training in Japan during the early 1960s. One night at his dojo, the Rembukan in Tokyo, Shimizu noticed a beginner standing around idle. So the sensei wandered over to ask why the student was not engaged in practice.

"I've got that last kata I learned down pretty well," the student said, "and I'm waiting to be shown the next one."

"Oh," said Shimizu, who then excused himself, saying, "I've got to go over here and practice some myself." Then the headmaster went to a corner of the dojo and began to go through the movements of *honte uchi,* the most basic strike of jodo, the first technique one learns when taking up the Way of the stick.

Of course, as we are constantly reminded, when it comes to self-defense, simple things are usually the most effective means for overcoming an opponent. Even if you are going to use more intricate or sophisticated methods in a self-defense situation, their success will depend largely on the attention you have paid to your kihon.

Now that we have considered at least some of the outer meanings of Funakoshi's advice that in simple things lies the key to victory, what about the inner, or ura, meanings of his maxim?

For a master of the budo, and for those who wish to reach such a level, attention to simple things means mirroring the lessons of the dojo in everyday affairs. When I read about Funakoshi or talk with those who knew and learned from him, I am struck by how unpretentiously, how *simply* the man conducted his life. The fame and renown that came to him in his later years when he was recognized as one of the luminaries of the budo world in Japan did not change Funakoshi. He remained an uncomplicated man all his life. (And so he was—again we are reminded of the essentially dichotomous nature of things, the omote and the ura—a very, very complex man.)

It would be worthwhile to keep in mind the example Funakoshi set for the budoka of succeeding generations, especially when we compare his lifestyle with the lifestyles of some of the more famous martial artists of today. Our martial arts celebrities are more apt to be talking about their latest movie deals than training in the dojo. They often package and promote their franchised schools with a kind of slick professionalism that is reminiscent of a used car salesman. And, not surprisingly, more than a few of these martial arts celebrities have found themselves in serious financial trouble and worse. At least two well-known karate teachers have served time in prison for dealing in illicit drugs. Others have been sued for all kinds of scams and confidence games involving dishonest tournament promotions, fraud, and the like. Less serious, but equally regrettable, are those martial arts promoters who get themselves mixed up in all manner of stunts and shenanigans designed to make a fast buck at the expense of the dignity and propriety of the budo. And so we have five-year-olds being promoted to black belt level mostly to draw coverage from newspapers, or TV news that will mean free advertising for the school, or events like world record board breaking feats that are ostensibly staged to promote a charity but that, are really only thinly disguised efforts at self-promotion.

The budoka who refrains from involving himself in these kinds of questionable deals and schemes may never sign a movie contract, may not run a chain of schools, may not, to be honest, ever make so much as a dime from his adherence to the Way. Yet, in keeping his attention focused on the simple things in life and on his budo, he has an excellent chance to attain a kind of success that more complicated people will never know about.

Chapter Twenty-nine

Subduing the Self

Thoughts of desire, fame, and profit are all human emotions, ones that often arise easily. It is not virtuous to indulge in them. To restrain these emotions, one should use the method of 'subduing the self.' Subduing oneself is difficult. We must summon sufficient willpower and not relent for a moment. We can maintain control over these emotions by being aware of their signs when they first arrive. This is the 'method of subduing the self.' If one determines to pursue learning and love what is right, thoughts of fame, profit, and material goods will weaken. If heavenly principles advance, human desires retreat.

—Kaibara Ekken (1630–1714)

I wonder what readers, contemporary martial arts practitioners, will think of the words written by Ekken nearly three hundred years ago. To one young karate champion I read about the other day who makes his appearances at tournaments accompanied by blaring music and hoisted on a palanquin, I doubt such words would have much more meaning than if I had left them in the original Japanese. For that kind of person, fame and profit were and will continue to be the very motivations that inspired him to take up one of the martial Ways in the first place.

And maybe that is okay. But there are also budoka out there for whom Ekken's words might resonate. They recognize that winning tournaments, inspiring adulation and gaining public notice are nice, but to pursue those diversions is never a worthy reason for following the Way. For budoka such as this, "subduing the self" has a profound attraction.

Now, lest anyone come to the mistaken conclusion that I am suggesting that rewards, monetary and otherwise, and the attentive respect of others are somehow inherently evil, I hasten to add that I do not have anything at all against profit or adulation. Those are both just fine with me. I will get paid for having written the words you are reading now. And people often—well, sometimes at least—say and write pleasant things about my writing. But when I think about my work, I am not thinking about the money I will receive for it, or the attention it might bring. I am concentrating instead on the ideas, the points I want to share, the subjects I want to explore and that I believe will be of interest to others. Now it is true that I might not be so keen to write if I did not receive a check for my work, or if everything that I wrote was either completely ignored or never raised any kind of response at all from readers. But getting paid or getting attention is not my primary reason for wrting. My goal is to be a good and communicative writer, to share with others some of the experiences to which I have been exposed in my years of following the martial Way.

What Ekken was talking about, has a direct application to our budo training. When we go to the dojo, it is, among other reasons, an exercise in subduing the self. We are engaged in exercises that demand the utmost concentration and effort. There is no time, in the heat of serious training, to think much about ourselves in an egocentric way. Committed budo practice tests us so severely that we forget about the possibility of winning tournaments, about the chances that we might one day star in action movies, about how much income we might make by someday teaching this art professionally. We are focused entirely on the perfection of the Way. (If we are not, then that is a very good indication that we are not training with the devotion or the intensity that is required of us.)

Of course, there is nothing wrong with success. But success is a by-product in arts like painting, or dancing—or the martial Ways. Concentrate on polishing your budo. In terms of your training, that is enough. Indeed, that is all that is proper in the dojo. Whatever else might come as the result of your budo practice, well, that will be nice for you. But insofar as your ego is concerned, for the true budoka, the goal of training is, as Ekken put it so well, subduing the self. And nothing more.

Chapter Thirty

Catching Catfish in a Gourd

The depiction of a catfish swimming around a gourd is a common motif in the art of old Japan. The whiskered fish and the gourd can be found as the subject of *zenga,* or Zen-inspired ink paintings that are usually artistic parables. The two even appear together engraved on *tsuba,* the hand guards of Japanese swords. Why? Even if I provide a hint—that a dried, hollow gourd was sometimes used to catch catfish—that doesn't really explain why the fish and the gourd trap have been so popular among Zen artists or why this motif decorates so many weapons. The answer lies in the way the gourd is used to snare the fish, and the meaning behind this fish story resonates in both Zen and martial arts training.

If you gave them a hollow gourd and told them there were catfish in the stream, some people, like me, for instance, would plunge right into the water, flailing away and trying to scoop up any nearby catfish so unwary as to show its barbeled face. This is an utterly futile strategy, of course. I have spent a great deal of time in rivers and sloughs where catfish hang out, and I have spent even more time eating them, and I can tell you that in their natural state they are among the most slippery of creatures on the planet. A catfish would slither and wriggle and die of old age or boredom before you could get it into a little opening at the end of a gourd. That would not stop some of us from trying, mind you—until we had been left exhausted by the effort, soaking wet and muttering about what an idiotic trap a gourd makes.

Others, however, would take a different approach. Give them a gourd and tell them dinner is swimming around in that stream over there, and they would sit and think about it for a while. Then they would wade quietly into the stream. Gently, they would sink the gourd so it rested on the bottom. Then they would go back to the bank and wait and probably get something else useful done while they were waiting—like getting the cornmeal and paprika and hot oil for frying ready. These people would be depending on the personality of the average catfish. If you live in a place that does not have them, catfish are curious fish. And territorial. If an unusual object like a gourd were sunk into the stomping grounds of the typical catfish, the fish would eyeball the gourd for a while. Then before long he would give in to the temptation to swim over to take a look at it. Before long, the mystery of what might be lurking inside that gourd in the form of a possible meal or an interloper would have to be investigated. Catfish are like that. The catfish would then swim into the narrow neck of the gourd to see what was inside— and then he would be trapped neatly as can be, unable in that narrow space to turn around and swim back out.

Now, our subject here is not oddball ways of catching fish. But it just so happens that the best way to catch a catfish in a gourd is very much like the approach you will want to adopt to learn certain skills in the budo. If you have spent much time in the dojo, doubtless you have encountered individuals like the catfish catchers I described first—the ones who leap into the water and thrash about with the gourd in their fist, madly trying to get a catfish to go inside, splashing and sloshing and cursing. Maybe you are one of them. They are the students who come onto the floor of the dojo with a furious intensity. The technique is demonstrated for the class, the students begin to work on it at their own pace, but these types are relentless about the task before them. "I'm going to get this if it takes all night!" That is their motto, of sorts. I remember one fellow like this who came to a dojo where I trained.

He would huff and puff, working so hard his face would take on the color of a ripe chili pepper and his keikogi would literally drip with perspiration. At each practice session the rest of us were always worried he was going to have a stroke right on the spot.

It is an admirable attitude, this sort of do-or-die enthusiasm. Unfortunately, in its raw, untempered form, it isn't worth much in the dojo. The problem is that even the simplest technique of karate, or aikido, or kendo, or any budo is not a matter entirely or even predominantly of physical skill. Learning the correct way to sit to begin class, for instance—on one's knees, back straight, weight balanced on the heels—cannot be achieved in a single class session. You can be *told* how; but your body needs time to "fit in" to the technique. It is not going to come overnight, no matter how determined you are, no matter how much energy you are willing to put into the chore. The catfish simply cannot be cornered and forced to go into the gourd.

The budo—and the catfish—are not alone in this regard. Could you, in the span of a couple of months, turn out a vintage wine, even if you had the best grapes, the finest winemaking facilities, and an unlimited production budget? Nope. The wine has to age and mature, and those processes take time. There are no shortcuts. Nor can this equation be changed regardless of how much "spirit" you can summon up for the project. The budo are a process. We are mixing analogies here, and all this talk of catfish and wine is making me hungry, but let us add another. The Way is constantly compared to a real way, a road or a path. This is a wonderful analogy. But we must remember that this particular road has its own distinctive geography, and the geography across which it takes the traveler is definitely not going to be confused with that of Kansas. At times, especially at the beginning of one's study, the Way is so steep and your steps are so unsteady that you cannot raise your gaze very far at all. Most of the time you can barely see where your next footfall will land. As you progress you may come to sections where things flatten out for a while, where you have insights that allow you a broader perspective. If you persist in your journey, though, it is going to get hilly again—you can count on it. There is no chance of seeing the destination before you have covered the whole of the route.

This is not to say that one should adopt a lackadaisical attitude toward budo practice. Unable to do even the most elementary of techniques perfectly, you may be tempted to despair, to rationalize that "I'm not going to get it right tonight, so why should I expend any real effort ever?" That is hardly a good frame of mind in which to come to the dojo. On the contrary, you must train with a total effort every time. Try as hard as you can, but at the final bow, let it go. Leave the gourd alone. The catfish will be trapped, just like the techniques will eventually come, on their own.

Obviously, it takes a lot of maturity to strike a balance here. You have to try hard, but you have to have the patience to accept that time is an essential ingredient, and as important as they are, effort and determination in whatever quantities cannot replace hours, months, or years of practice. It is not easy to be patient. As I said, the attitude "I'll get this right tonight or I'll die trying" is useless for learning or mastering the budo—in its raw form. But that attitude taken and diluted with a heavy dose of patience will result in a spirit that is absolutely necessary to training—"I'll get this right— maybe not tonight, but some time before I die."

Catching a catfish in a gourd may not be the most cost-effective way to bring home dinner. But it works. And in the long run, it is a method more efficient than chasing that fish all over the stream and ending up with nothing but wet.

Chapter Thirty-one

Rinkiohen ("Moderation")

During the seventeenth century in Japan Yagyu Hyogo no suke Toshiyoshi was a respected swordsman of the ryu of martial arts that was founded by and named after his family. His technique with the sword was reputed to be superb, fearsome. But in addition to his skills as a swordsman of the Yagyu Shinkage ryu, Toshiyoshi was famous for his amazing health and boundless energy. His strength seemed almost beyond that possible of a normal person. If local legends are to be believed, the mountains near his home were filled with supernatural beings like hawk-nosed goblins and other such creatures. Some of those who knew Toshiyoshi wondered if he had consorted with these beings and learned some secrets of vitality.

Unlike the leaders of the main branch of the Yagyu school of martial strategy, Toshiyoshi was not employed by the Tokugawa shogun at the capital in Edo. He was the fencing instructor to Tokugawa Yoshinao, the lord of Owari Province. When he was not teaching, Toshiyoshi liked to play the game of *go,* and he lived a quiet life. Even so, because of his skills with the sword he was sought out by aspiring martial artists who wished to learn from him and to gain the secrets he was supposed to possess for strength and vigor. One of these young exponents, a warrior from a neighboring fiefdom, was so persistent in his requests for instruction that Toshiyoshi finally consented.

Toshiyoshi told the young Mitsuru, a samurai from a high-ranking family, that his personal servant had requested a leave of absence, to go home to visit his father who was ill. If Mitsuru would fill in as servant, assisting Toshiyoshi with his daily chores, the master would give him lessons.

Mitsuru was delighted. He accompanied Toshiyoshi everywhere and watched his every movement. He was determined to learn the secrets behind Toshiyoshi's abilities and, by imitating them, to become strong and fit himself. He noticed that Toshiyoshi ate only vegetables at mealtimes. No fish or meat. He saw that the sword master took his bath in the morning rather than in the evening, unlike most people who liked to relax in the steamy heat of a wooden tub at the end of the day. He also noted that Toshiyoshi spent a couple of hours every evening reading until he retired to bed.

By the end of a month, Mitsuru was certain he had discovered the secrets of Toshiyoshi's energy. He returned to the service of his own lord believing that what he had learned about diet and daily routine from Toshiyoshi was more valuable than the basic techniques of swordsmanship that Toshiyoshi had taught him. The young samurai eliminated meat and fish from his diet. He switched his bath time from the evening to the morning. And, like Toshiyoshi, he applied himself to reading works of philosophy each night before sleep. Over a year passed, and although Mitsuru was nowhere near as strong as Toshiyoshi, he was patient and knew he was on the right path. Then he was sent back to the mansion of Tokugawa Yoshinao on an assignment for his clan and was reunited with Toshiyoshi there. Upon this second visit Mitsuru was immediately struck by the differences in Toshiyoshi's behavior. This time when he ate a meal with the master, Toshiyoshi was enjoying plates of grilled fish and other kinds of seafood. He was taking his bath in the evening, not in the morning as he had before, and instead of reading at night before bed, he was going for long walks in the countryside.

"Your habits are entirely inconsistent!" Mitsuru exclaimed in frustration. "Why have you changed your routine completely?"

Toshiyoshi shrugged. "Sometimes I like vegetables, especially when they are in season. But just now the fish is fresh and delicious. As for the baths and walks in the evening," he continued, "I take a bath in the morning in the summer because it makes me feel clean and refreshed during the hot day. In wintertime a hot bath at night keeps me warm while I sleep. During the warm months, I don't like to exercise after I've bathed, but in the winter, a walk in the brisk air feels good and helps me go to sleep quickly."

"What then is the secret of your health and energy?" asked the disappointed Mitsuru.

"Rinkiohen," replied Toshiyoshi. "Moderation in my daily habits, along with steady and consistent training in strategy and swordsmanship, keeps me healthy. These are my only secrets."

I was reminded of Toshiyoshi's approach to health when, not long ago, a young karateka I know confided in me concerning a most embarrassing problem she was having. It is not the most pleasant of subjects to consider, but it is one that is becoming increasingly common in our society, particularly among young people. She complained to me that she suffered from frequent bouts of diarrhea, and, further, nothing she tried seemed to help. She was on a special diet and taking a couple of different medications for her ailment, but it refused to go away. She was growing so worried about it that she was afraid to leave home to go on trips or outings, and she could not even attend a movie or a concert without the nagging fear that she would have to make a frantic dash for the restroom at an inopportune moment.

I suspect that my friend is far from alone. In this bustling world, our minds and bodies are under tremendous stresses, sometimes from sources of which we are not even aware. Physicians note that ever-increasing numbers of their patients are complaining of headaches, diarrhea, constipation, and vague feelings of nausea. Ever ready, the drug manufacturers and others in the health care business have come up with all kinds of potions and advice. It is nearly impossible to watch an hour of television or flip through a magazine without coming across advertisements for special diets or preparations to fix up our unhappy insides. Unfortunately, except for those unusual cases when these conditions are brought on by some physical infection or disorder, although the various diets and medications may help things temporarily, eventually the problems return.

I asked the karateka some questions about herself. I knew that she was a top student in college who spent many hours studying, often staying at her books all night before a big test, and that she felt that such sacrifices were absolutely necessary to her education. When she did have a chance to sleep, it was for exceptionally long hours, and she ended up missing meals. When she did eat it was at irregular times, and she was so afraid of the diarrhea being aggravated by certain foods that she had become quite picky and would eat only those foods that she believed would help her overcome the illness. She admitted that when she wanted to relax she went to parties and drank beer.

In many of her daily habits, the collegiate karateka thought she was helping herself. But she was actually ignoring the probable cause of her illness in the first place. Research has shown that the long hours of "cramming" that high school and college students do is not nearly so useful to them as are much shorter periods of study, planned well in advance with plenty of breaks. Likewise, psychologists generally agree that the regularity of our sleep is nearly as important as the amount we get. It is also wise to try to get the right kinds of foods every day. But excessive worry about diet (or anything else) can be a major reason that the digestive system begins to malfunction. And to seek out relaxation only on particular occasions through the use of alcohol or drugs can, of course, hardly be considered a healthy lifestyle choice.

What, then, can my karateka friend do to help herself? She can follow the advice of Yagyu Toshiyoshi concerning the practice of rinkiohen. He would tell her, no doubt, to regard her diarrhea as her body's way of warning her that she is under stress and that she is not getting the proper kind of rest or nutrition. Then the master would tell her to try to balance her lifestyle a bit more carefully, getting regular sleep whenever possible, eating a wide variety of foods at regular times, and to realize that illness, like occasional colds and other such irritations, is a part of life for everyone, unavoidable at times and not necessarily a reason for great worry or a serious threat to her health.

It goes without saying that we cannot rid ourselves of all sicknesses just by balancing out our daily activities and engaging in moderation in our habits. Serious or prolonged symptoms are always best brought to the attention of a physician. As more and more of us struggle, both in the dojo and outside it, to make our way in the world, though, the simple advice of Toshiyoshi has a meaning worth consideration. "Moderation in my daily habits, along with steady and consistent training, keeps me healthy. These are my only secrets."

Chapter Thirty-two

The Luxury of Anger

According to the thinking of many of the swordsmen of old Japan, there were four basic "sicknesses" to which the martial artist could fall victim. The sicknesses are fear, doubt, worry, and surprise. Many of the spiritual elements and much of the psychological training in the budo now, as then, has been directed at overcoming or preventing these illnesses. To that list of four I think it might be wise to add one more affliction that is just as deadly and insidious as the other four. To that list I would add the sickness of anger.

"A man is like steel," goes a Japanese proverb (and the advice applies equally well to women, I hasten to add); "once he loses his temper he is worthless." My sensei had a different, rather more direct way of expressing the same sentiment. He brought it to my attention one afternoon when he was teaching me out in a meadow below an old cemetery near his home. We were practicing with wooden swords. At that time in my training with him I was experiencing a phenomenon every serious budoka has encountered at one point or another. I was forgetting the kata. I had reached a stage of learning where sections of the different kata I had been taught were getting muddled in my mind. The movements of different kata were running together. Even more infuriating, during the execution of the sequence of a particular kata all of a sudden I would draw a blank. Some of these movements I had been doing regularly for more than a year or two, and suddenly, to my tremendous frustration, they were gone, vanished from my brain. My body would stop as if my nerves and muscles had short-circuited. It was maddening. It was especially hard to bear for someone like me who has a pathetically low frustration level. It was even worse because when I stalled, Sensei, who was acting as my opponent in the kata, would simply stand there, expressionless, waiting for me to execute a technique I could not for the life of me produce.

"*Shimatta zo!*" I finally snapped in exasperation at my own stupidity.

Sensei's response was so fast it was completed, over, long before I realized it had started, in less time than it took me to complete the interjection. He snapped his wooden sword against mine and flicked it over, using the powerful force of his hips, in an action that took my weapon right out of my hands. My sword wheeled over in the air a few times and bounced off the ground. Simultaneously, I was left with the distinct sensation that my wrists had just been yanked off of my forearms.

"Anger is a luxury," he said quietly. "One that you cannot afford."

Anger as a luxury item. That is a curious way of thinking about that emotion, isn't it? But, as with most of the advice my various sensei gave me right after they'd captured my attention in similar and equally painful ways, it is worth thinking about.

Anger is a luxury because it allows us to focus our attention on only one thing: ourselves. Remember back to the last time you stubbed your toe or lost your keys or wanted to stomp that gas pedal right through the floorboards when the car wouldn't start? At such moments nothing else in the world was on your mind but *your* immediate problem. Anger, in that sense, is very much like your mind taking a little vacation. When you take a vacation, you have the luxury of going for a swim or a hike, reading a book loafing around all day if you like. Anger may not be quite so enjoyable (nor does it include the healthy benefits of a vacation), although few would deny that it *is* a satisfying way to "let off steam" when we are really irritated, just as I did with my imprecation out in the meadow when I couldn't remember the kata.

When I lost my temper I indulged myself. I focused on my problem, forgetting all about my opponent. On the battlefield, the place where those kata were intended to be implemented, that kind of self-indulgence could have cost me my life. As a budoka, the price I would have to pay for the luxury of getting angry was too dear.

Sometimes we may wish to believe that anger "pumps us up." If the goal is simple enough, maybe that is the case. If I have to kick down a door, get me angry enough and I will probably be able to do it. But the physical, combative skills of a martial art are not simple. One must be aware of distance, timing, the actions and reactions of an opponent, the possibility of encountering more than one attacker, and so on. In such a complex situation, anger has no business.

Another belief about anger—and we see this quite often in films and other forms of dramatic entertainment—is that it can motivate us to be brave under situations of great stress. Again, in some limited instances, this may be so. But depending on anger as a source of energy can have some serious consequences over time. Anger involves the adrenal glands in the body. This may not be the most scientific explanation, but the adrenals squirt their juices into us in moments of stress or danger or anger. What follows is a complex process, but the upshot is that blood pressure, heart rate, respiration—all these functions go into a quick overdrive. It is as though the body is a family station wagon, one that has not been started in a while, which is suddenly turned over, revved with the pedal to the floor, and then driven as fast as it can go, all in a matter of seconds. If there is an emergency and you have got to go somewhere fast, it is nice to have transportation that can get you there. If you try that with your car on a regular basis, though, it will not be long before the engine and transmission are in trouble.

Those whose professions depend on violent or dangerous encounters—soldiers, policemen, and firefighters, for instance—soon learn of the negative consequences of depending on an adrenaline-fueled anger to meet these situations. The body can handle occasional bursts of anger, but when anger becomes a conditioned response to stress, cardiac surgeons start scrubbing up. As a species, we have not evolved, chemically or emotionally, to remain healthy under this kind of stress. No more than the family wagon was designed to be cranked over and raced at full throttle when the engine is cold. (The Chinese, incidentally, noted long ago some of the more subtle problems we encounter when we are too angry too often. Taoist medical texts from centuries past refer to this as an imbalance of "fire" *chi,* or *ki* as we would put it in Japanese, and many forms of *tai chi chuan* and *chi kung* practice provide special exercises to rid the body of this excess energy.)

Anger wastes energy indiscriminately, usually at a time when we need to preserve energy and use it to maximum benefit. It focuses concentration very narrowly in moments when we need to be more cognizant of what is going on around us. It robs us of self-control precisely when we most need to be in control of ourselves. It would be idealistic to hope that through training we could completely eliminate the anger that is sometimes within us. In my own case, I don't hold out much hope of that happening. But if our budo training cannot eliminate our anger, it can teach us to recognize what our anger is really all about, and to see that more often than not it is an emotion that we can ill afford to indulge.

Chapter Thirty-three

Shooting with a Broken Bow

The bow is shattered; arrows are all gone.
At this critical moment—
Cast aside all doubt.
Shoot without the slightest delay.

So goes a poem written by the Zen master Bukko Kokushi during the Kamakura era (1226–1286) in Japan. It is typical of Zen-inspired poetry, isn't it? By which I mean, of course, it is more than slightly puzzling, bordering on the nonsensical at first reading. At second reading, too, for that matter, for how can we shoot our bow when it is broken? And what are we supposed to shoot anyway, if all our arrows are gone?

Kyudo, the Way of the bow, is the Japanese martial Way of archery. It is a modern evolution of *kyujutsu,* the military art of using the bow as a weapon of combat. Kyudo is one of the less popular forms of the budo, especially outside Japan. In the West, exponents of this art are still somewhat rare as compared with followers of the other martial Ways; good, high-level teachers are almost nonexistent. That so few individuals seek to take up the Way of the bow is not really hard to understand. Equipment is exorbitantly expensive. A good *yumi,* or bow, handmade of laminations of bamboo and various woods, can cost more than a thousand dollars. Then, too, the essentials of learning to shoot the bow according to the precise dictates of kyudo are so exacting that at times the art seems to have more in common with the tea ceremony than with a blood and guts fighting discipline. The kyudoka spends months learning the intricate etiquette of *kyu-ha,* the rituals of the bow. The details are daunting. All of them must be committed to memory until they are integrated into the kyudoka on a level that is virtually instinctive. There are a fixed number of steps taken to approach the shooting stand, for instance. The angle at which the bow is held while the arrow is nocked to the string must be just so. All imaginable facets of the mechanics and movements of drawing and shooting are precisely set into forms that have been formalized now for many, many years. The forms must be learned exactly. There is even a predetermined series of standardized motions established for approaching the target, leaning the bow against it, and pulling out arrows that have already been shot there. Kyudo is a budo form not long on external action, to say the least.

Although kyudo is more formal in its approach than are karate or other forms of budo, the practitioner of any form of the martial Way will recognize that a lot of attention is focused on what seem to be petty details of their art. Before he came to the dojo, the novice karateka probably assumed he could throw at least a halfway decent punch. Once involved in the study of karate, however, he discovers he cannot even make a simple fist correctly, not according to the demands of that art. His shoulders have to be adjusted by the teacher, his chin tucked in, elbow pulled back, and on and on. Once I observed a beginner's karate class and counted the technical details given for performing a basic reverse punch. The teacher gave no less than twenty-four different instructions in one lesson. There were twenty-four details to remember while carrying out the most fundamental action of punching. I have seen novice karateka become so overwhelmed by the demands of the art that they actually freeze; one can see in their face and eyes that they are so frantically trying to remember it all that they cannot even move!

In kyudo the attention to all these external details is referred to as *toteki.* Among those who are uninformed in the subtleties of the art, there is considerable criticism about this approach to training for a "fighting" art. Those who lack experience or an informed exposure to it make all manner of ambitiously ignorant commentaries on the toteki to be found in the budo. They often suggest that in a real fight the martial artist who has participated in the process of toteki will be so concerned with getting his stance right, his posture correct, and so on, that he will be pounded into the ground by an attacker before he can make a single motion in his own defense. This reasoning is based on the misassumption that the toteki stage of training is the *final* goal in the journey of the budoka. But toteki is just a stage.

As time goes by in the dojo, the kyudoka begins to integrate the details of the art into his performance. He no longer has to mentally count the steps as he approaches his place on the shooting stand. They come out naturally. The arrow nock finds its way to the string without conscious effort. This is the stage of training that the kyudoka calls *zaiteki.* At zaiteki, the bow and the archer are becoming one. Budoka studying other forms of the martial Ways may use another expression to mean much the same thing. They will speak of *mushin,* a term borrowed from the nomenclature of Zen. *Mu* is "nothing," or "without." *Shin* means the "conscious" or the "mind." "Without consciousness" or "no mind" is an approximate translation of "mushin"—and this serves to demonstrate how poorly many budo concepts can be rendered into a foreign language.

The image that springs to mind when we hear this translation is not something most of us would want to emulate in a dangerous situation—that is, unconscious or having lost our minds! What "mushin" refers to, though, is a state where the budoka is not conscious of the details of his technique. (Those who follow the Ways of calligraphy or the tea ceremony are looking for the same quality in their practice.) The budoka who has grasped mushin behaves naturally, spontaneously, no matter what the situation. He has passed through the level of his training that required him to concentrate on technique. The quality of mushin is indicative of achieving a level of training where technique has become so integrated, physically as well as spiritually, that it can be consciously left behind. The technique is "no-technique," if I may indulge in some Zen-speak myself.

While this description smacks of pseudo-mystical mumbo jumbo, it is not beyond the everyday experiences of nearly all of us. If you can type, play the piano, drive a car even, you know something of mushin. There was a time, in typing class or at piano lessons, when you looked at the keyboard, studied it, and tried to get your fingers to move to the right spots. You had to concentrate on each letter or note. Gradually, you began to make connections, to create words or tunes without thinking. If you continued on, you reached a stage where you did not consciously need to direct your fingers to the right spots. They "knew" where to go on their own. In fact, if you are a skilled typist or pianist and someone asks you about the layout of the keyboards of either instrument you would probably be stumped. Which keys are on either side of the *J* key on your computer or typewriter keyboard? You may be able to type eighty words a minute, but you probably can't say. That is because you have attained a certain mushin in typing, you see. You have gone beyond technique. There is nothing mystical in your ability. Just practice.

(There is, I hasten to add, a vast difference between the "no-technique" of the expert budoka and the "non-technique" of the beginner. Neither the neophyte typist nor the skilled secretary who types eighty words a minute may be able to tell you what adjoins the *J* key. But that does not mean they are the same in terms of their understanding and mastery of typing, does it? One must strive to get to the point of no-technique, and there is no shortcut, no way to bypass technique altogether.)

The bow, the arrows: as the Zen master's poem reminds us, these are external details. Drive yourself past them, using the techniques, the external details, through severe, unceasing training and effort. Press on into the core of the art. When your budo is fully integrated in body, mind, and spirit, the bow and arrows, the details of the punch or kick or strike or throw, are not important. At the critical moment, as Bukko advised, you must penetrate the target without the slightest delay.

Chapter Thirty-four

The Squirrelly Approach to Budo

In terms of the study of Chinese philosophy, the "neo-Confucianists" were those thinkers who came after and built on the ideas that were laid out by the great sage himself. The values and the theories of learning articulated by some of these scholars have had a major influence on the development of Japanese culture and specifically on the budo of Japan. One neo-Confucian philosopher was Hsun Tsu, who wrote about the innate nature of man, about the working order of the cosmos, and about the nature of reality itself. Hsun Tsu was a contemporary of another renowned Chinese thinker, Meng-tsu, better known in the West as Mencius. These two, thinkers, Hsun Tsu and Meng-tsu, are, in fact, considered the Aristotle and Plato of early Chinese thought.

Hsun Tsu is known for his expressive writing style and his eclectic interests. Typical is his comparison of some human beings to squirrels. "The squirrel can do five things," Hsun Tsu wrote. "He can climb a tree, swim, dig a hole, jump, and run. All these are within its capacities, yet it does none well."

Now let me preface this discussion by saying that I do not mean to imply that my fellow martial artists are squirrelly. Still, it does occur that Hsun Tsu may have been giving some advice about the task set before those who start out to follow the budo or any of the other related Ways like flower arranging or calligraphy. Let us compare it for the moment with another bit of mammalian counsel with which you may be more familiar. In C. W. Nicol's delightful account of his karate-do training in Japan in the early 1960s, *Moving Zen,* he tells of his frustration with trying to keep up his judo practice while at the same time making an effort to train regularly with the Japan Karate Association. Doing both, he found himself constantly exhausted, and never fully recovering from minor injuries. Finally he confronted one of his JKA teachers with the problem. In response, Nicol was told that "a hunter who chases two rabbits at the same time will catch neither."

Today Nicol's book is a classic in martial arts literature, and many budo teachers like to quote the hunting advice Nicol received when their students come to them to discuss adding another Way to their martial arts studies. Sometimes the advice is sincere; other times I suspect it is pompous and self-serving. When a teacher is afraid of losing a student or wants to get out of demonstrating or teaching skills in another martial art in which he claims dishonestly to have mastery, he can simply try to look wise and repeat the admonition about rabbit hunting. But we are led to wonder if Nicol's sensei was not voicing the same sentiment in a different way than Hsun Tsu did centuries ago. If we budoka extend our training efforts in different directions, do we risk missing our target? Does Hsun Tsu suggest we will end up like the squirrel, adequate in a number of endeavors, master of none?

One answer to these questions might be found in the writings of Kanze Zeami. Zeami was a sixteenth-century master of the ancient Noh theater of Japan, its first great figure, and the founder of a school of Noh drama that continues today with one of his descendants serving as its current headmaster. A performance of Noh, if you have never seen it, is an example of an intensely ritualized and formal art. With very rare exceptions, you must go to Japan to see Noh. When you start feeling sorry for yourself as a budoka, when you start to feel that there are so few real experts in the martial Ways to learn from outside of Japan, then you may count your blessings that it was not the theater art of Noh that grabbed your attention. If you want to study Noh, you virtually have no choice but to pack your bags and go live and train in Japan.

Fortunately, much of Zeami's writings on Zen have been translated and are available in English. Those budoka who have not read any of his work should do so as soon as possible. Most of the legendary sword masters of old Japan appreciated Noh, and more than a few of them were connoisseurs of the art. They had a particular insight into its methods of movement and timing and spacing, since those concepts were vital to their own combative skills. What Zeami wrote about Noh, all of it, can be read from the perspective of the budo as well. Any serious budoka will find a lifetime of study and contemplation and reflection in Zeami's words about Noh. Zeami quotes Hsun Tsu's remarks about the squirrel, in fact, and explains that the aspiring Noh actor may find himself in the same situation. He may try to improve his art in every area, only to succeed in being mediocre in all of them. So, too, with the aikidoka who takes up kendo or the karateka who begins to study judo. Zeami's solution to this problem is expressed in one of his writings:

> As the result of persistent training, untutored style will develop into greater artistry, constantly improving until, before he knows it, the performer has reached a level of versatility and exactness. If his training is comprehensive and he expands his art in versatility and magnitude until he attains full competence, he will find himself at the level of the flower of truth.

I think what Zeami might be saying is that the various facets of Noh theater performance will appear entirely disparate to the beginner. The complicated, dancelike gait patterns, the chanting, the difficult movements—none seem interconnected to one another, at least not in the mind of the beginning student of Noh. So, too, the *ukemi* (breakfalls) of judo, the *tai sabaki* (body shifting) of kendo or aikido, and the *atemi* (strikes) of karate all seem like completely different and unrelated concepts to the budoka who is just starting his study. The student's "persistent training," Zeami suggests, must be in mastering the fundamentals of one art. That kind of practice, pursuing one rabbit, will bring the budoka to a high level of competence. He cannot stop there, though.

After gaining "versatility and exactness" in karate, Nicol went on, as his book explains, to take up *iaido,* the art of drawing and cutting with the sword, and, later still, he became involved with *jodo,* the art of the stick used against the sword. He was following the advice of Zeami, expanding his art "in versatility and magnitude."

We have squirrels digging all year long in the flower gardens outside the dojo where I train. They occasionally wreak havoc with some bonsai that sit on a shelf near the door. They sometimes scamper loudly across the roof during meditation before and after our training. So I hope they don't get any better at those particular skills. But I try to be a bit squirrelly in my own approach to the budo, using the lessons of one Way to assist me in understanding another. Learning the etiquette of bowing in the tea ceremony taught me a trick for moving rapidly during practice of aikido's *suwari-waza,* or "seated techniques." There is a way of placing your hands on the mat during the tea ceremony that will make clear the position in which you need to keep your hands when you are coming up off the ground in the advanced karate kata *Unsu.* It was from a practitioner of Japanese dance that I learned how to make the basic stepping and turning motions and the single-legged rotations of the kata *Hangetsu.*

Learning Noh is not going to make you a budo master. Learning to play the *shakuhachi* flute will not mean you can automatically pick up a sword and draw and cut with it like an iaido expert. What will happen, if you increase the breadth of your explorations into the culture and thinking of Japan, is that the depth of your budo will increase correspondingly. You will see, as Zeami did, that all the Ways are very much interconnected and that all of them can be instrumental for budoka who seek to attain Zeami's "flower of truth."

Chapter Thirty-five

Woodcutter's Karate

If you have not spent a spring in the midwestern region of the United States where I live, you have missed out on witnessing one of nature's most impressive and dramatic annual displays. As soon as the weather warms up and the moist air from the Gulf starts to shove its way into the Mississippi Valley, we have our thunderstorm season. Most of these storms pop up in the afternoons of April, May, and June, when the rays of the sun have heated the atmosphere all day, creating updrafts that spill out clouds larger than a county, thunderheads full of wind and lightning, and brief, torrential rains.

Those who are not natives can be disconcerted by a midwestern thunderstorm. My nana, from Nova Scotia, would come to visit but she never did get used to the storms. She would fret and stew and jump with every crack of lightning. My karate sensei were almost as twitterpated when they first came to the midwest. I was practicing in a quiet cemetery one afternoon in May with one of them, when, without warning, the sun was blotted out by a giant cloud the color of a fresh bruise. From a far distance, thunder rumbled. My sensei held up his hand to stop our practice. His native island of Okinawa gets few of these kinds of storms. When he heard thunder, his first thought was of a typhoon. I explained that the chances of a typhoon in Missouri were rather remote. If the storm did reach us, I told him, we would have warning enough to walk back the couple of blocks to the house where he was living. That afternoon was more than two decades ago. But sometimes in the spring when I hear distant thunder, I am reminded of that day, the feel of soft, newly green grass tickling my bare feet, the electricity of the storm building in the air, the joy of learning this wonderful art from my teacher.

It was in May again, one of the first thunderstorms of last summer, and I was sitting in my office at home trying to finish an article on the computer before the fingertips of lightning that were all around reached out and snapped off our power. There was a sudden blast of wind that shivered the house, a pause, and then a splintery *crash!* from outside in the dark that ended in a terrific thud. There is—was—a giant mulberry tree in my neighbor's yard, one with three trunks joined at the base, two of which have been dead since before we moved into our house. One of the three had become a casualty of the storm. By a miracle of wind direction, the dead trunk missed landing on the gardening shed with my collection of bonsai inside it, but it did hit our fence, crushing the aluminum top rail like a paper clip. The bulk of the dead trunk dropped right between our yard and our neighbor's.

My neighbor and I stood in the rain together, surveying the damage by flashlight. He has dogs that could get out without the fence to keep them confined. (I would have been happy to have seen them gone; they are barkers set off at all hours of the night by who knows what, and I would not have missed them a bit. But if they left his yard it would be to get into mine, where doubtless they would leave numerous reminders of their presence for me to clean up.) There was nothing to do but to cut the trunk in half and prop up the fence to keep the animals in. We waited until the rain had tapered to a drizzle. Then I got out my axe and took a whack at the downed tree. The first blow I struck sounded less like hitting wood and more like I was banging against the metal fence. The wood of the mulberry was so old it was nearly petrified. The axe plinked off it like it would have bounced off concrete. Our second plan was to saw notches in the trunk then chop at the exposed wood, which we hoped would be softer. My neighbor brought his weapon out, a long carpenter's saw. I got mine, a double-edged Japanese saw.

My *nokogiri* (the generic word for saws in Japanese), with its bamboo-wrapped handle and flimsy-looking blade, didn't look like much next to my neighbor's hefty tool. Not only does a nokogiri look different from a Western-style saw; it is used very differently. The Western saw cuts on the push stroke; the nokogiri cuts on the pull. The saw is powered by the shoulders; the nokogiri is driven back and forth by the strength of the hips. The saw is clutched like a pistol in the clenched grip of one hand. The nokogiri is held lightly, with both hands, exactly the way one would grasp a Japanese sword.

The drizzle soaked us both as we worked in the dark. Before long, I heard my neighbor begin to pant, then gasp, then grunt with exertion.

"I gotta take a break!" he finally groaned. He stopped and straightened, rubbing his sawing arm. Now I need to point out that my neighbor, an auto mechanic, is much bigger and stronger and a little younger than I am. So I cannot say any of those advantages—strength, size, or age—were on my side as I kept sawing after he had to quit. The reason I kept going, I realized as my nokogiri continued to bite into the old mulberry trunk, was because I was using the same body mechanics I had learned in the dojo.

The stance of the *shokunin*, the traditional Japanese craftsman, is very similar to karate's *fudo-dachi*, or "immovable stance." My knees were flexed, allowing the large muscles of my hips and abdomen and thighs to do the work. In contrast, my neighbor sawed primarily with the muscles of his upper body, in his shoulders, with his posterior sticking out as he worked, the way a white belt's does when he is learning to punch. I kept my torso perpendicular to the earth, my body moving back and forth as a single unit. In a number of important physiological ways, I realized as I sawed, the most effective body mechanics for making a front kick are also the most efficient ones for cutting through a log.

I was concentrating on the pull stroke of the saw as I worked, the *hikite,* the karateka calls it, the hand that retracts, adding power to the thrust of his punch. I was paying attention to my *ibuki,* the cycle of my respiration, and rather than holding my breath and then grunting with the effort, I was breathing naturally and keeping my inhalations low against my diaphragm. Instead of using a saw that forced me to turn away at an angle from my work and use only one arm, I used my two-handed nokogiri, which allowed me to face the trunk of the tree fully and to use both arms in harmony. I am not a shokunin. I'm not even a good home handyman. The Mount Fuji cone of dry mulberry sawdust on the damp ground below my nokogiri was not growing because of my woodworking skills; it was, because of whatever mechanics of motion I had managed to learn in my years of training in the budo.

The mulberry trunk, felled in seconds by a gust of wind, gave way much more slowly, but just as inevitably, under the teeth and edge of my neighbor's saw and my nokogiri. I would not recommend this exercise as a regular substitute for budo practice. But I did notice the next morning that I had aches in many of the same muscles that suffer after a strenuous training session at the dojo. Soaking in the tub that night, I also had the satisfaction of knowing that I could answer with a "Yes, I have" if someone asked, "Have you ever used your martial arts training?" And if I am ever asked how many boards I can break, I can truthfully say, "Hey bud, in my martial Way, we don't break boards. We go for the whole tree."

Chapter Thirty-six

Hiyameshi ("Cold Rice")

The stories of Gichin Funakoshi's early days of pursuing the art of karate in the last part of the nineteenth century sometimes have an element of the melodramatic about them. Each day, after finishing his work, he would walk from his house to his master's house, a little more than five miles away, along a lonely country road in the backwoods of Okinawa. The path he took through the thick, junglelike forest was so dark that when night fell he had to carry a lantern in order to see his way. Once he arrived at his master's place he would train hard for a couple of hours and then, relighting his lantern, Funakoshi would retrace his journey in reverse, arriving home again just before dawn, in time to go back to work during the day as a schoolteacher.

At about the same time Funakoshi was making his nocturnal hikes to study karate on Okinawa, on the mainland of Japan Jigoro Kano had finally found a place to practice *jujutsu*. To be more exact, he was in the process of creating the martial Way of judo that he envisioned as a natural evolution from the older methods of jujutsu he had learned. His new, makeshift dojo was a dilapidated Buddhist temple, Eisho-ji. Unfortunately, the floor of the temple was as rickety and weak as the rest of the structure. The floorboards could barely hold up the sections of *tatami*, Japanese straw matting, atop them. The bodies slamming about on a daily basis did not do the floor any good. Long after the other practitioners had left for the evening, Kano and one of his senior students would creep into the crawl space beneath the floor, ignoring the cobwebs and dust, to repair the structure well enough so that it would last through another training session.

The live-in disciples of aikido's founder Morihei Uyeshiba often found that the demands of aikido training were the least of their everyday problems. Because of their master's eccentric ways, they were regularly roused in the middle of the night to serve as bleary-eyed opponents for Uyeshiba, who would have a flash of martial inspiration in the evening and would immediately want to try out whatever technique he'd dreamed of. His live-in students would take the role of an opponent for Uyeshiba, attacking him with full force even though they could barely open their eyes. In addition to their training, they had to tend the gardens and farm plots on the Uyeshiba property and carry his baggage when he went away on long train trips. Invariably, when Uyeshiba's original students are asked to recall their early days with the master, they will describe these activities, which left them utterly exhausted.

And you and me? We ignore the aches and pains of daily training and practice. We push aside the concerns of a day of work or school; we resist the urge to settle into an easy chair with a good book or a video. On one more night, we set off for the dojo, to be thrown about, punched and kicked at, and God knows what else. The majority of us endure the rigors of training for no easily explainable reason. We are mature enough to know the budo are not going to make us movie stars, or invincible warriors, or wealthy. Yet we continue on, through stifling summers and winters so cold our feet go numb against the cold wood of the dojo floor. We have deliberately chosen a path, a Way, that takes us over a course of suffering where the reward for working oneself through the physical and intellectual maze of a kata or a technique is to have another one heaped on, another one to try to absorb. And the further we travel on this path we are on, the more demanding it becomes. Errors and lapses in attention that may be forgiven when we are beginners are illuminated in a harsh spotlight by our teachers as we progress.

Finally, as we approach the stage of expertise where our teachers and seniors have no more to teach or to criticize, we might think the journey is nearing completion. Not so. At this level the budoka is expected to turn inward, to relentlessly examine his technique and his whole lifestyle, searching out any weakness, imposing upon himself ever more hardship, seeking a level of the Way that is increasingly severe.

This austerity, known to all practitioners of the Ways of Japan, from calligraphy to the budo to the tea ceremony, is called in Japanese, *shugyo*. But among budoka it is more colloquially known by an ironically descriptive term: they often call it *hiya meshi o Michi*, or "the Way of eating cold rice."

If you do not prepare rice as a part of your regular diet, you may wonder at such an odd expression. The next time you have some leftover steamed rice in the refrigerator, give it a taste before you rewarm it or put it in the microwave. You will find the texture and consistency of the rice is, well, less than palatable. It's lousy, in fact. It is tough, bitterly starchy, and unpleasant to chew, very different from fluffy, warm grains fresh out of the pot. Soldiers in the field must eat their rice cold, because they lack the equipment or time to heat it. Bachelors who subsist on take-out dinners and wake up in the morning with nothing for breakfast but leftovers eat cold rice, too.

Sometimes, though, when circumstances dictate that a person must eat a bowl of cold rice, he will take it willingly. He may use a meal like that to remind him of the simple, humble things in life. A bowl of cold rice can serve to make a person appreciate that even the most blessed and fortunate among us must sometimes suffer. Not every meal we eat can be tasty or hot or prepared exactly as we would like it. Despite its texture, cold rice is just as nutritious as rice that is fresh and hot. Eating cold rice can be a way of putting food in perspective. If we are hungry enough, cold rice can be satisfying, and it can provide us with the sustenance that we need even though it does not satisfy our tastes. The austere practice of the budo is much the same. It is a discipline stripped of self-indulgence, of ego decorations. To follow a martial Way requires a certain amount of stoicism and an enduring spirit. The budoka prefers cold rice, so to speak, because he sees it as an essential means of improving himself, a means of perfecting his spirit.

It is not exactly accurate to say that the budoka "prefers" cold rice. More to the point, he *accepts* it, believing as he does that if he spends his life always looking for and demanding comfort and ease, he will never be tested, he'll never be pushed to refine his body and spirit. The budoka accepts the hardships and austerity of cold rice because he feels that true contentment is not to be gained by acquiring things. If you cannot be satisfied and happy unless you have hot rice with every meal (or a new car every year, or the latest fashions in clothing), you are apt to spend a whole lot of your life unsatisfied and unhappy, since for most of us, having all these things is just not possible. But if you can find happiness in your rice whether it is hot or cold, chances are you will find the same contentment in everything life has to offer you.

The great budo masters of the past ate plenty of cold rice in their day. They suffered and endured. Their lives were not without happiness or good times or other luxuries. But none of them created lives that were centered on materialistic goals. They chose a different path, a Way that means accepting some hardships. The late author Malcolm Muggeridge once said that all of the valuable lessons he learned in life he learned through suffering. Likewise it is hard to imagine that the great budo masters would ever have attained what they did without a stoic outlook. Those of us who have elected to follow in the Ways they have left for us must come to our own conclusions about in what directions we want those Ways to take us. Wherever we choose to go, however, if it is to be along the path of the budo, we must be prepared from time to time, to eat some cold rice.

Chapter Thirty-seven

Bend Like the Bamboo

Bend like the bamboo. Be flexible; give before the onslaught of force in the same way the long slender boughs of that giant grass flex in the wind or under a load of snow. Remain supple and spring back against oppression as do the bamboo's stalks. This concept of giving, of demonstrating flexibility against force, is one of the basic precepts of the Japanese martial Ways. Practitioners begin hearing this advice as soon as they enter the dojo. In fact, even those who have never practiced a budo are familiar with the example presented by the ever-yielding bamboo. In dozens of self-help books and seminars and articles, the theme of gaining more satisfactory relationships with others (in our age this is generally synonymous with the notion of "getting your own way" in a manner that is socially acceptable) is described as a kind of social or corporate judo, one in which power is gained by giving and remaining supple, emotionally and mentally.

The bending, flexible bamboo is such a familiar metaphor for both the martial Ways and for everyday life that it can be easy to forget that the majority of Westerners who write and talk about it, as well as those who try to understand it, have never actually *seen* much bamboo as it grows and lives in nature. Very little bamboo is grown in the United States, so few students here have had an opportunity to watch this remarkable plant do its stuff, to see its boughs flex, gathering their loads of snow and then sloughing it off to spring upright again. Just as someone would not fully grasp the meaning of "watch for the high, hard ones" if that person had never faced a fast-firing pitcher from the batter's box, "bending like the bamboo" can be a foreign concept if the only bamboo you have ever seen has been in the shank of a fly rod.

A couple of years ago I planted a stand of yellow-groove bamboo in a square of ground in my yard. I had done some work repairing a tea hut in the Japanese garden of a nearby botanical garden, and in return the resident horticulturist dug up several clumps of the bamboo along with their inter-laced wads of rhizomes and gave them to me. I stuffed them into the rear of my little Honda hatchback and started home. It wasn't long before I was stopped by a policeman. The green stalks of bamboo and their lacy leaves must have looked suspiciously like another plant, one that, had I been car-rying a carload of it, would have been of considerable interest to the officer. I made it home without being arrested, and I planted my bamboo.

The climate of central Japan is quite similar to that of the part of the Midwest where I live. So I knew the bamboo would survive just fine. But I was surprised when the clumps I planted immediately shot out a half dozen new shoots. I was amazed by the speed with which they grew. During the morning I would use a string to measure the growth, then I'd check it again in the afternoon to find how much it had pushed upward. The phenomenal growth rate of bamboo is legendary, but it is astounding to see firsthand a shoot gain more than two inches in the course of a day.

I watered my bamboo all summer when the ground was dry. In the evenings of the autumn that followed, I listened to its feathery rustle against the wind. I was waiting to see how the bamboo would fare when the snow came. Finally, on the morning of the winter solstice—the word for that day in old Japanese is *toji*—the weather was abruptly cold, and then the sun van-ished. Fat, menacing clouds the color of a tarnished nickel had covered it. By the time I finished reading the paper that morning, heavy flakes were falling. By afternoon the branches of my bamboo had grown a thick white coat of snow. They were bending, lowering beneath their load. Completely

distracted from my writing chores, I brewed a pot of tea and sat in the din-
ing room, looking out the window at my crop of bamboo. If you have never
seen it, snow-burdened bamboo doesn't just sag with the extra weight; it
twists over alarmingly. It goes down as if it is suddenly developing the
advanced symptoms of some kind of plant arthritis. Smaller stalks will bend
double, their tips arching right over into U shapes that touch the ground. Just
when I began to doubt the plants' pliancy, just when I was ready to rush out
and knock the snow off to save the plants from snapping, one length of bamboo gave a convulsive shudder. It shrugged off the snow, then, after staggering
and waving back and forth, it was upright again. Then another, and another
repeated the process, and pretty soon and they were all loosing the snow that
was piled on them, swaying back upright like drunkards wobbling unsteadi-
ly to their feet.

All winter I watched the bamboo I'd planted as it flexed under successive
snowfalls and then flung off the weight. Spring came and more shoots erupt-
ed from the cold, black ground. I had read stories of the Taoist sages in
China who would celebrate the season by drinking tea and munching on
fresh steamed bamboo shoots, so I made tea and ate some of my crop. But
even with my appetite, I could not keep up with the new growth. Bamboo,
I had been warned, can take over a yard faster than a greedy land developer
can turn wetlands into a shopping mall. The neighbors were beginning to
suspect I was keeping a panda in the house. I decided it was time to do some
pruning. I started by digging at the base of one of the clumps. And that is
when I learned there is a whole lot more to the pliant strength of the bamboo
than what you can see in its snow-covered branches. Bamboo, propagates
itself by rhizomes, long fibrous roots that spread out horizontally a foot or so
underground. These roots expand and intertwine, forming a netlike web. The
rhizomes are incredibly tough. Even with a sharp spade it took a very long
time to chop through the root system of the small section I wanted to dig out.
I finally resorted to using a Chinese meat cleaver to get the job done.

As I noted, the yielding bamboo is a familiar image that can be found in
all kinds of analogies from all over Asia. But flexibility is only half of the

bamboo's strength. The stalks of bamboo are supple, true. They can bend into incredible curves without breaking. Yet without the stout, deeply entrenched roots below ground, the stalks would topple with the slightest resistance. People who know only of the bending and flexibility of this unique plant are not aware of the rigidity that makes real pliancy possible. With the bamboo, flexibility is possible because of the strong, tough roots at the base of the plant.

This lesson about the bamboo plant has some important implications for the budoka. It is all well and good to try to meet an attack in a spontaneous way, for instance, flowing and yielding, loosing your attacker and then snapping back like the bamboo in snow. But this strategy is useless unless you are thoroughly rooted in the basics of a fighting art. The master is able to improvise with creative flexibility and come up with spectacular techniques, but if a less talented practitioner were to try these moves he would end up looking like an addled cow. The master's success at improvisation is a result of the years he has spent perfecting basic body movement. The would-be originator of his own combat system will soon discover that his techniques won't bear up under the pressure of an attack unless his roots are already sunk in a well-established art.

I wish bamboo was grown more widely in this country. When I visit Japan I always take the time to find a grove of it and wander through at my leisure, listening to the sounds and enjoying the sway of the stalks in the wind. My own stand of yellow-groove bamboo has grown so lushly that each spring I have friends (and even a few complete strangers who have shown up at the door asking about it) who come to take their own clumps to start bamboo groves of their own. It is a beautiful plant, and if more of it were growing in the United States, budoka would have a chance to see in real life the plant that gave rise to the analogy they've encountered so often. But more to the point, they could more completely understand the lesson of the bamboo's strength: flexibility, a true kind of suppleness that allows one to bend and spring back against opposition, is merely an illusion unless there are firm and solid roots to anchor it.

Chapter Thirty-eight

Mirume ("Looking to See")

The eyes in combat, wrote the eccentric samurai Miyamoto Musashi, must take in everything and nothing. The swordsman Negishi Tokaku, founder of the Mijin ryu of martial arts, recorded in the scrolls containing the essence of his ryu that the most effective gaze for the warrior in combat is one directed to the opponent's fists as he grips his sword. Many other martial arts exponents have written or spoken about the proper focus of the martial artist's eyes, advising everything from the quite practical to the mysteriously obscure. Yet invariably these writings concern themselves with the *heiho no metsuke*, the fixing of the gaze during combat or as it relates directly to martial strategy. What about what might be called the *tsune no metsuke* of the budoka, that is, the ways he looks at things in his everyday life?

In daily life, training, working, relating to others as we make our way in the world, the budoka strives to adopt the attitude of *mono o mirume*. In the parlance of everyday Japanese, this phrase can mean simply "to look at things." Yet it has a deeper connotation, meaning "to look *into* things." This expression has a special significance for those who follow the martial Way, but it applies as well to artisans in all the traditional arts and crafts of Japan. When a potter examines a ceramic bowl, he looks at the glaze on it and he sees the outer form of the bowl, just as an ordinary person examining that piece of pottery would. Yet as an artist, he looks deeper. He sees into the essence of the bowl. The famous potter Shoji Hamada, whom I have mentioned before, once said that when holding a bowl he could "see its inner formation and see, too, the character and shape of the individual who made it." Hamada was talking about seeing the pottery with the gaze and the attitude of mono o mirume.

Years ago, I was at a festival of native crafts in a little town in the Ozark Mountains. An old fellow was displaying the use of the broadaxe, a wide-bladed cutting tool that was a necessity for building a house when the components of that house began as lengths of felled trees. The broadaxe was used to square off freshly cut timber so it could be stacked into the walls of a house. The man at the festival was demonstrating how this squaring off was done by straddling a thick white oak log and skillfully shaving off the sides in quick strokes with the razor edge of the axe. A woman watching remarked that she admired "that rough-cut" surface he was making.

"T'ain't nuthin' rough about it," he replied. He pointed out that the timber he had seemingly hacked square with random blows of the axe was actually well planed with a series of even notches and slashes. He was revealing an adroitness with the axe that must have taken him years to perfect—as well as demonstrating his eye for recognizing the inner form of the log before he ever struck it with the tool. He was a master of the broadaxe, a man who knew how to look at an object with the gaze of mono o mirume.

Traditionally, students of an art or a Way in Japan do not look directly at the lesson being given for their benefit. In the dojo, for instance, trainees may lower their gaze slightly when watching a technique demonstrated, or they may focus their vision at a place just past where the action is. The disciples of some schools of martial arts are encouraged to watch what's going on from *sanpaku,* which means "one third white." This expression refers to positioning one's head in such a way that it is fractionally tilted down so the bottom third of the eyeball, the white beneath the iris, is showing.

This may seem like a silly thing to do. It sounds impractical at best. After all, if we want to study and learn a technique, we have to watch how it is done. But remember, we're talking about looking mono o mirume—not at, but into. Sometime when you are injured or recovering from an illness, or when you can go to the dojo but for some reason you cannot train, it will be of benefit for you to watch to see how others learn. You can actually learn a great deal yourself this way, especially when you watch beginners to see how they respond to new material that is presented to them. You will observe that most of the time they are not using mono o mirume. They look *at* the technique, but they don't see it.

A good example of trying to learn by looking at a technique occurs when beginning karateka try to copy the front kick they have just seen their teacher demonstrate. They have looked at the kick; that is, they have seen the foot somehow swing up and land at head level, and that is what they will clumsily set about to imitate. It will not be until much later that they will see into the kick, concentrating not on a specific point, but taking in the whole motion indirectly. Then they will be aware of the cocking of the knee, the chambered thigh and calf, the pressing thrust of the hips, the vital flexing of the support leg. They will see more than just a foot striking or a collection of the disparate parts of the kick. They will appreciate the kick as a complete technique.

Focusing directly on an object tends to localize our perception, to reinforce previously formed judgments. New karateka kick so awkwardly in part because they tend to equate kicking with their only other likely exposure to the activity, usually kicking a ball. Relying on that narrow experience, they do not grasp the very different methods used in the execution of a front kick. They are like the fellow who looks at a tea bowl and concludes, "Hmm, damned poor beer mug." He is not seeing the tea bowl, only a drinking implement that fails to measure up to his narrow standards.

Mono o mirume goes far beyond observing an object or a simple action, as you have probably guessed. A spouse snaps at her husband irritably. He hastily concludes, "She must've had a bad day." And he hurries off to escape the unpleasantness, never pausing to look more deeply, to try to fathom the reasons for her anger. A grandson listens with half an ear to the seemingly endless stories his grandmother tells him of her youth, but he never stops to think that her stories are a rich source of wisdom for him. A karate practitioner goes to the dojo for his lessons week after week, never once stopping to consider the possibility that his art is anything more than a sophisticated form of battery. Unfortunately the world is filled with individuals who are satisfied by seeing only the surface of things. Budoka, though, those who would follow the Way as a lifetime journey, should keep their eyes on the path before them. Every day. Not just a glance now and then, but a long and deep look into things. Mono o mirume.

Chapter Thirty-nine

Even If I Die

Yasuhiro Yamashita was one of the most remarkable champions in the history of judo. Back in 1977, when he was just nineteen, Yamashita became the youngest competitor ever to win the National Judo Championships of Japan. The chubby-cheeked Yamashita went on to capture a stunning nine consecutive championship titles (no other judoka in the history of judo has won more than three). During his years of competition he compiled a record of 528 wins and just 15 losses and 15 draws.

Yamashita is still a popular figure in Japan, even now that he is retired, both because of his success as a judo competitor and because he is considered an outstanding role model for young people in Japan. Plainspoken yet respectful and kind spirited, Yamashita is the sort of hero American lads used to find in baseball players in the days before too many of those athletes began devoting the bulk of their energies to salary negotiations, narcotics, and vulgar behavior off the field.

I followed Yamashita's career avidly, and I was always impressed by his attitude toward judo and competition. Once, after he captured still another national title, I recall something he said that, to me, seemed to sum up Yamashita's philosophy on competition and said a lot about his successes. "Just before a tournament," Yamashita told reporters, "I always take a bath, and in the weeks before competition I try to keep my surroundings neat and well-ordered, so I won't be ashamed even if I die during a match."

Think about that quote for a moment, if you will. It is really quite remarkable. "Even if I die..."

During the feudal age, it was a habit of the samurai on the eve of battle to bathe himself with ritual care and to attend to all sorts of details in the eventuality that he did not survive the next day's fighting. He wrote letters to loved ones and sent clippings of his hair home so they could be preserved at the family altar. He would comb and arrange his hair carefully so that if he died, his corpse would be a little less unsightly. Samurai often went to the trouble of burning incense in their helmets before a battle—so that if they were beheaded, the remains would at least be pleasantly perfumed. The classical warrior entered a fight, in short, with the attitude that he would not survive it. He abandoned any thought of living and concentrated his spirit on facing death.

It is very, very difficult for us today to understand the mentality of the feudal Japanese warrior in this regard, since we are separated from him and his world by so much time and distance. Even the modern Japanese often have a vague and frequently inaccurate conception of how the samurai felt about death. Unfortunately, the single best known commentary on the samurai's approach to death is to be found in the *Hagakure*, a collection of the advice of Yamamoto Tsunetomo. Yamamoto was a samurai retainer in the service of the Nabeshima clan late in the seventeenth century. In 1700 the lord of the clan, Nabeshima Mitsushige, died of natural causes. Yamamoto made known his wishes to disembowel himself, to follow his master into the next life. Earlier in Japanese history, this sort of sacrifice was not uncommon. *Junshi* was the term for suicide performed to join one's lord in death. By Yamamoto's time, though, the practice had been outlawed by the ruling Tokugawa government. (Not that there is much that could have been done to punish someone after he had died. Nonetheless the laws prohibiting junshi did discourage self-sacrifice, because they dictated that if a samurai were found to have illegally killed himself, all the records of his accomplishments and even those of his ancestors would be destroyed. This was serious business to the warrior class, and its threat no doubt stayed many a hand that would have otherwise reached for the dagger.)

Instead of dying, Yamamoto became a monk and lived in religious seclusion for the rest of his life. His thoughts on the Way of the samurai were recorded in handwritten scrolls by an acquaintance and later published in book form as the *Hagakure* (Hidden in the Leaves.) In this work Yamamoto observed that "the way of the samurai is found in death." This is a dramatic statement. It was later quoted to young kamikaze pilots to encourage them to sacrifice themselves during World War II, and it probably would have been effective, one can easily imagine, to goad Japanese citizens into throwing themselves in front of the invading U.S. forces had not the war ended before such an invasion could take place. But dramatic though the sentiment is, it does not really reflect a pervasive attitude about death held by the samurai of Yamamoto's time, not by any means. Yamamoto—and this is significant—was never in a battle. Not even a personal duel. So his words about sacrificing oneself have to be taken in context.

I think a much clearer representation of the Japanese warrior's concept of death was explained by Otake Risuke, the current head instructor of the Katori Shinto ryu, one of Japan's oldest schools of martial strategy. Otake has described the samurai ideal as a person determined "to leave something behind and then to be able to throw away the human body and to accept death." The samurai, like the budoka of today, did not tend to think of death as a convenient end. He regarded it as a daily reminder that we all have a brief moment in the world to accomplish what we will. Death could come for us tomorrow or many years hence. We've no way of knowing when. And so we must throw ourselves into daily life as if each moment could be our last. For the feudal samurai, that meant serving the interests of one's lord, completely and with utter loyalty and commitment. What does it mean for the budoka of this century?

Today, most of those who follow the martial Way do not—thankfully— have to put their skills to the ultimate test of combat. *Shiai shobu,* the tournament match, is very unlike a life-and-death encounter. Still, if one is to enter competition—given that the budo *are* in a profound and fundamental way an encounter with life and death—it must be with an attitude of utmost sincerity. Many budoka who compete in judo, karate, and kendo have come to approach the contest aspects of these budo forms as if they were a game. They are unaccustomed to thinking in terms of living and dying. They are more comfortable with lesser, more pedestrian concepts such as winning and losing. If they seek the true budo, however, they should never enter into these contests in the spirit of sport. Nor can there be any concern for the scoring of points or for protecting a lead until the clock runs out. The budoka can only settle the matters of life and go into the competition as if he is approaching his death. That is exactly what the judo champion Yamashita did during his brilliant career.

Facing death, allowing into one's consciousness the thought that this performance might cost someone his life no doubt seems contrary to current popular theories about sports. Experts on the subject of what it takes to win these days tend to suggest that competing athletes focus on "positive imaging," conjuring up mental pictures of winning that are supposed to influence the contestant favorably, so that when the tournament day comes the athlete will be able to translate the daydreams of his imagination into real victory.

How can we reconcile these two concepts: the popular notion that positive imaging is the way to win versus the notion of confronting death with each instance of combat, the way Yamashita did? I don't know. But I have a clue. Positive imaging, like the idea of budo as a sport, is a modern notion. Yamashita's view, which calls for just the opposite attitude—contemplating the very worst possible outcome and planning ahead for it—is based on the belief that the budo are far more serious than sport, that within the teachings of the budo there is something to be grasped that is more valuable than just winning.

The budo *are* more than sport. They are a Way of life, one that, as champions like Yamashita Yasuhiro know, can only be traveled completely by facing death.

Chapter Forty

Formalities

After morning practice at the dojo yesterday I had to go to a funeral. No, we didn't kill anyone in training. My practice and the funeral were not related. At least, I didn't think they were.

Sitting at the funeral service, it occurred to me that a good many of the mourners did not know how to behave on such an occasion. Some were dressed more appropriately for a game of touch football or for cleaning out the garage than for a funeral. Others were hesitant about approaching the casket or unsure about expressing their condolences to the family. This sort of social vertigo is, unfortunately, all too common in our age. I have seen the same uncertain behavior at virtually every other event in my life that might be categorized as "formal," at weddings, at school commencements, and so on. Brides receive applause now as they stand beside their new husbands in churches and synagogues, as if they were entertainers who have just performed well. As they step up to take their diplomas, graduating seniors at high school or college are greeted with howls and whistles and other noises that would seem to belong in the bleachers at the NBA finals. Some would argue that there is nothing too terribly wrong here. Such behavior is explained away by the notion that people are merely reacting naturally. "Formality" is dismissed, within the parameters of this argument, as artifice.

Thus, being informal is not just permissible; it is a sign of mental health. People behaving in an informal way are people being themselves. But having watched the discomfort of those attending the funeral, I must disagree. The informal attendees at that event were not behaving and dressing as they were by choice. They simply did not know how to conduct themselves under the circumstances.

The assumption that all formality is fake and contemptuous and limits the free expression of the self is one of the more lamentable curses of our times. What is worse, it is a curse that we have inflicted upon ourselves. By confusing formality with "snobbishness," decorum with pretension, dignity with egalitarianism, we have dispensed with etiquette and standards of behavior in nearly every facet of our lives. Perhaps we did get rid of the snobbishness and falsity by choosing informality. But we have lost something else as well, haven't we? We have lost a sense of decorum and dignity, and, more important, we have lost the self-confidence and courtesy and respect for ourselves and others that are hallmarks of all worthwhile civilizations.

In my opinion, one of the most significant (and most often overlooked) qualities of the traditional budo is that they offer a method of rediscovering and recovering a sense of formality and all the positive attributes that go with it. When I trained at the dojo the morning of the funeral, we bowed to the *kamiza* shrine to begin practice. We bowed to one another. In performing the *kata*—we were practicing iaido, the art of drawing and cutting with the sword—we knew which foot to move away or toward the shrine; we moved so that our weapons in their scabbards would not accidentally clash, we avoided walking in front of others who were sitting or standing. There were dozens of actions we undertook that morning in the dojo, as we do each time we practice there, and all of them are designed to meet the standards of correct etiquette—formality.

I offer two observations on the formality of training in the budo that may be of interest: first, our behavior in the dojo in no way interfered with the process of training. We were not moving about like automatons. We were not so concerned with getting every little aspect of etiquette correct that we had no time to train. The perspiration was flowing liberally. It was a tough workout. In the dojo, learning the proper etiquette, called *saho* or *reishiki* in Japanese, is a process that unfolds over a long period of time. It is an ongoing process for the budoka, incrementally introduced. If he is being taught properly, the student in the dojo is never so overwhelmed with rules and regulations of etiquette that he finds it impossible to move. He is taught slowly about manners and the formal way of doing things in the dojo. The lessons are integrated into his training, so they emerge naturally, with a perfect economy of motion. Second, the bulk of the manners exercised, the demands of formality that are required for training in a traditional dojo, are so subtle and so intricately woven into our behavior while training that the uninformed visitor will, in all likelihood, not even be aware that the budoka are exhibiting these manners.

Some of our formalities, shared with generations of martial artists who have come before us, have practical origins. Walking around a sword that has been laid on the floor, for instance, is a courtesy to its owner, but it is also, from a purely pragmatic point of view, safer than stepping over it. Other rituals of dojo etiquette, such as bowing to one another, encourage a sense of concern and appreciation for fellow practitioners. And still other conventions of dojo manners, such as our treatment and behavior toward the dojo shrine, are reflections of the deep sense of the spiritual that pervades all serious budo training.

Formality is very natural in the dojo, even though it is something that must be acquired through careful and expert instruction. After being immersed in it on a daily basis, it becomes, as I said, automatic, a reflex. It is never stultifying, never phony or stiff, at least not to my way of thinking. Some may disagree. They may insist that a latitudinarianism is more expressive of tolerance of the many different backgrounds and lifestyles represented in the dojo. They might maintain that informality is conducive to a more comfortable learning environment. Maybe they have a point. But a lot of the most skilled budoka I have known, regardless of their ethnic or social backgrounds, have submitted themselves to the strict impositions of traditional budo etiquette. They have learned—and extremely well in some cases—under quite formal circumstances, and the formality does not appear to have hampered their education in any way that I can see. The martial artists whose training has been conducted in an atmosphere of formality gain something more as well. They carry that sense of decorum and dignity with them when they leave the dojo. It is not snobbishness or arrogance or antiegalitarianism. It is a calmness, a sense of self-assurance. Formality does not intimidate them, and at times when it is necessary for them to maintain a formal bearing, they do not have to "put it on" or behave stiffly or unnaturally. Formality is a part of their everyday lives as a result of their budo experience, so for the budoka formality is a part of their sense of their own true self. Obviously, one can acquire this familiarity with formality without ever having followed the martial Ways. But I wonder: can one hope to be a serious budoka without it?

Chapter Forty-one

Sabi-Shiori, The Art of Being Alone

What is it that makes the budoka? What, if anything, is the primary quality that distinguishes him from the general population? I do not mean here, of course, anything like technical competency or physical prowess. Nor do I intend to imply by "distinguishes" a kind of superficial celebrity status. Let us for the moment dismiss the arguments about whose techniques are the most lethal or the most authentic or who has been privy to the most arcane secrets of the mystical East. And let us agree that the number of martial arts magazines a person's snarling visage has graced, the videotapes in which he has starred, the Hollywood luminaries under whose shoulder-hugging arm he has been photographed—these are not reliable indices for the quality we are talking about. When I am asking here what it is that makes the budoka, I am entertaining an entirely different idea. What I mean instead is the quality, that character that we see in a rare budoka now and then that leaves us thinking, "That guy is what the martial Ways are supposed to be all about," and wondering how it is we can attain that quality ourselves.

In my opinion, the essence of that quality is difficult to name exactly. Yet it is ever so simple to explain in the way in which it is manifested in the character of the budoka. It is generated and nurtured, I believe, through the process of *sabi-shiori.* What does this expression mean? It is better to explain it through examples. The practitioner of iaido, alone in the morning cold of the dojo, drawing and striking with his sword, then returning it to its sheath. The karateka who appears at the training hall on a snowy evening to practice his solitary kata when no one else has ventured away from his warm home. The aikidoka who goes off by himself, taking his jo into the woods and practicing the movements that connect him, according to the principles of his art, to the movements of the universe. These are examples of sabi-shiori, a term borrowed from the idiom of Japanese aesthetics. It is best, though awkwardly, translated as "solitary aloneness."

Sabi-shiori for the budoka is a state of mind, really—or, to be more precise, a state of the spirit. It is the recognition that the Way of the budo is inherently an isolated highway, one that leads the traveler on a solitary journey. Even if we are in the crowded midst of a hundred other practitioners at a training seminar or with the dozen or so dojo mates with whom we regularly attend class, our efforts are individual in the martial Ways, intensely so if we progress very far at all. Solo practice, then, is not a change from regular training. It is the normal state of things in the life of the budoka. And although the expression "sabi-shiori"—solitary aloneness—might seem to connote a sadness, a melancholy to be avoided if happiness in life is the object, it is a concept that actually indicates an acceptance of the solitude that much of life brings. Embracing the spirit of sabi-shiori implies a willingness to accept solitude, to use it as an invaluable means of self-development.

Sabi-shiori is also a willingness to take the lessons of the regular classes in the dojo to a higher level. The budoka who is drawn to the budo at this level cannot settle for what is explained in training lectures or teachings that are readily available in books about the budo. He willingly delves deeper, on his own, knowing that the true secrets of these Ways must instead be experienced, worked and woven into the soul. If he is puttering about in his garden, the grip he has on his rake is the same one he uses to hold the sword or staff. Pushing a child in a swing, he moves from the center of his body, the power of the motion emanating from his hips. Reading a history book, he relates the struggles of civilization to what he has learned about the strategy of the martial Ways.

Daily life for the budoka traveling the Way with the spirit of sabi-shiori works the other way, too: not only do the activities of his life provide an opportunity for him to practice his art; his art is also incorporated into and revealed in his life on a day-to-day basis. He strives to be gentle and confident in his actions, to be sensitive to others, to act and react from a position of calmness and strength no matter what obstacles he encounters, in matters as trivial as navigating a traffic jam or as crucial as facing his own death.

Probably somewhere in your own life between the trivial and the crucial, in fact, you have met this kind of budoka and he has inspired you. By that I mean that we tend to run across such people not when we are specifically looking for them, but when the circumstances are just right. We are not in a crisis in our own lives, exactly, yet we know there is something missing. There is a gap that needs to be filled, a compass heading toward which we know we need to be steering ourselves. And then we encounter a budoka of this extraordinary caliber and we grasp that we have found a model, a guide. We do not, despite romantic tales, find a budoka such as this off living by himself as a hermit. The pursuit of sabi-shiori is not an end in itself. Aloneness, the sense of being solitary in order to follow the Way, is not a worthwhile goal in life. Instead, the sensation of sabi-shiori encourages us to be alone frequently better come to know ourselves better. As we uncover these greater insights within, we are more capable of returning to the busy world and being with others in a successful and meaningful way. This state of being is the hallmark of that rare budoka who inspires us. Next time you encounter a person of such a caliber, try to find it, this presence of sabi-shiori, which is inevitably at the foundation of the gracefulness and kindness and quiet strength that mark his persona. See if you can perceive the part of this budoka that—even when he is in the middle of a crowd—is always alone and at home with himself. This is the part of his spirit that will compel him to go to the dojo by himself and walk the path of the budo in contented solitude. If you can see that part of him, then you will have a glimpse of sabi-shiori. And if you are serious about your own journey along the martial Way, you will use that kind of budoka as an example for your own trip. Watch him and learn from him, and then you will be ready to set off on your own path of solitary aloneness.

Chapter Forty-two

Are You Ready?

I was reading an interview with the wonderfully talented potter Toshiko Takaezu the other day, and one of her comments was the sort of observation that stays in your mind, a thought so simply and yet eloquently stated that you recognize it has implications far beyond the matter the person happens to be talking about at just that moment. Ms. Takaezu, a Japanese-American, was describing the time she spent studying the tea ceremony in Kyoto in an effort to polish her understanding of the ceramic utensils that are used as part of that art. She was engaged in training in the tea ceremony at the Urasenke, the oldest of the established schools of the art. One day, while attending to some chores in the offices of the school, she overheard Sen Soshitsu, the current headmaster of the Urasenke ryu, who was talking to a Buddhist priest who was interested in beginning a practice of tea. Soshitsu spoke with the priest at length, Takaezu recalled in the interview, and then Soshitsu told the man bluntly, "You are not ready as a person to make tea."

That is a thought-provoking comment, isn't it? It becomes even more so, and more cogent from our perspective as followers of the martial Ways, if we substitute for the phrase "make tea" the words "do budo." Are there some people who are not ready to commence a practice of the martial Ways?

I do not mean "ready" in the physical sense, of course. We are not referring to a failure to meet the minimum levels of muscular strength, stamina, or body coordination necessary for the practice of the budo. I mean instead what I think Sen Soshitsu meant when he spoke with the priest who wanted to begin a practice to tea; I mean an emotional and psychological fitness, a standard of *spiritual* readiness to take up the journey of the martial Way. Regrettably, this is a consideration that will surprise some exponents of karate, aikido, and the like. This breed of practitioner I'm talking about believes that advancement and expertise in the martial Ways come purely from excelling in violent confrontations or winning contests once one has learned to be effective with the techniques of the art. For these individuals, the budo will exist solely in a physical plane. The spiritual and mental dimensions of the martial Ways will remain unknown to them—or more accurately, I would venture to say, these practitioners may suspect that these other dimensions exist, but they are so intimidated by the spiritual and mental realms that they will never make an effort to explore them.

These practitioners remind me of some of the different factions of European society before the great age of discovery, back in the fifteenth century. There were those who just didn't give a damn about the possibility that there existed other lands and other civilizations beyond their own. There were those who knew of the possibility but who, from fear of the unknown or from a selfish desire to maintain the status quo, ridiculed and tried to suppress the idea of exploration. (I must admit that I have a special disdain for these types, because there are still plenty of them around today. Lacking guts and imagination, they seek to dismiss or to deny the existence of these qualities in others.) Finally, there were those who possessed the depth of intellect and courage to pursue, to push off into the deep and forbidding waters in search of new knowledge and the chance of magnificent rewards.

Today the budo tolerates those who wish to practice only at the physical level. It suffers those who downplay or ridicule the more profound reaches of the Way. But it rewards those intrepid enough to follow the Way with sincerity, to make their way toward its most distant and difficult to reach destinations. These are the sort of budoka who, as the tea master Soshitsu might put it, are ready "as people" to do the budo and to make it a fundamental part of their lives.

From the conversation Sen Soshitsu had with the priest, the potter Toshiko Takaezu learned a lesson she considered extremely important for her work in ceramics. "I realized," she said in the interview, "that in order to make good tea bowls, manual skill is not enough. One must turn inward and try to develop inner human qualities for this work."

By her own account, Ms. Takaezu was well into middle age before she began this journey inward. As I admired her work at a recent exhibition, it was easy to see that her efforts at improving herself had contributed to the perfection of her art. Her insights should be of interest to all artists, especially those of the martial variety. We who are on the path of the budo should be asking ourselves, from time to time, "Am I ready as a person to follow this Way?"

Chapter Forty-three

The Spirit of *Enryo*

In the traditional budo of Japan there are certain attitudes that consistently prevail. Budoka generally do not enter into involved discussions of these attitudes, either among themselves or with outsiders. They do not discuss them with each other because these attitudes are expected to be learned by a kind of social osmosis in the dojo, communicated without words. Budoka do not discuss them with outsiders because it is very difficult to express them in words even to the initiated, and there is a sense that "those who are capable of understanding it will, without being told." So budoka tend to take these attitudes for granted, and, more to the point, seasoned budoka will pass them along to the next generation not through any kind of formal instruction but rather through their own actions. It occurs that those outside this legacy might be interested in learning more about these attitudes. With the arrogance of the writer, who is convinced he can explain intellectually that which is essentially inexplicable *via* the intellect, then, I approach the subject of *enryo*.

Enryo may best be described as "emotional reticence" or "stoicism." At the outset of this explanation, I need to stress that those for whom enryo is truly an integral part of their training and life do *not* demand that others subscribe to enryo as an "approved" form of behavior or way of living one's life in and out of the dojo. If others who come from different cultural traditions wish to live with a different attitude and code of conduct, that is, of course, their right. When enryo is a vital part of the budokas' character they wish only to follow their own path in terms of their own behavior and approach to life and to allow others to do as they wish.

A good example of enryo is the way the budoka expresses his emotions during *shiai* or competitions related to his martial Way. At some of these competitions it is now common to see participants who have won a bout punch the air in victory and jump up and down with joy over their success. Losers storm and stamp about and display all sorts of anger and frustration and disappointment. Winners acknowledge the adulation of the crowd. Losers sulk or protest. Both may embrace one another after a hard-fought match. None of these displays of emotion or feeling will occur at contests involving traditional budoka. The spirit of enryo pervades. Without looking at the signals of the referee at the end of such competitions it will be impossible to tell who has won; both competitors will be that perfectly stoical. (If you ever have an opportunity to watch a match of sumo, you will see enryo at a kind of rarefied and perfected level by these men, perhaps the last professional warriors on earth, engaged in contests in which enormous sums of money, prestige, and even physical well-being are at stake. Yet their faces, in victory or defeat, are the essence of passion concealed.)

Enryo had its origin on the battlefield of the samurai. Today we have what are appropriately called *shiai shobu* "tournament contests." In the days of the samurai, though, it was a matter of *shinken shobu,* "a fight with live blades." Scoring a point in that kind of situation meant inflicting a serious, possibly lethal wound against an opponent who was trying very, very hard to do the same damage to you. Your job, as a samurai, was to protect the interests of your lord. Even with death at hand, you could not forget your primary task in a fight: take out the enemy. To show your opponent that you were hurt or frightened or angry or frustrated ("scored on") was to give him a dangerous advantage over you. "Show him nothing" was believed to be the warrior's best strategy. Keep him guessing about how badly he has hurt or intimidated you. Make him wonder if you might be superhuman, or cause him to doubt his own ability, even for a second, and the advantage was yours.

Defeating an opponent, on the other hand, could also present other dangers. Concentrating on cutting down one enemy could distract you from another who was coming up behind and planning his own attack on you. The expression used by the samurai, "in victory, tighten your helmet cords" was not entirely figurative. Not at all. A samurai whooping around in a victory dance or a show of exultation could quickly be cut down. To be alive at the end of the day, to continue to breathe and to be upright and capable of taking nourishment, was enough of a celebration for him.

If they have been trained correctly and with the proper feeling, budoka today will inherit some of the spirit of the classical samurai. Budoka are also influenced by the philosophy of Zen Buddhism, a doctrine that began to exert a strong influence on the budo late in the nineteenth century. Zen addresses a number of questions about the way in which the budoka ought to approach his life and to contemplate his death. Contrary to some widespread misconceptions, Zen does not teach an indifference to life and death. It insists, rather, on putting life and death in perspective. What does it mean, in the space of an entire lifetime, to have won or lost a particular tournament? What is the value of such a victory measured against the important goals of a life well lived? These are some of the questions Zen may raise for the serious budoka. Concern for winning or losing, especially after the matter has been decided, is not "wrong," the philosophy of Zen would instruct. It is merely irrelevant. Both the winner and the loser will be contemplating what they did during the contest and how they might improve the next time. But there is no need for any display of emotion once it's over. To indulge in demonstrations of disappointment or celebration is to risk ignoring what is going on *right now* and to avoid dealing with the present. What the outsider might see as a kind of coldness or impassivity on the part of a budoka is really a full participation in the moment at hand.

Enryo, this affinity to stoicism, and to reticence, this constant sense of control over the display of emotions (and control over the *display* is not at all the same as controlling the emotion itself) is not merely an attitude, a way of behaving under certain circumstances; it is a way of living. Not the only way of living, the budoka understands. But it is a way full of history and meaning and a deep resonance of spirituality. It is the one he prefers.

Chapter Forty-four

Not Knowing, But Doing

A budo colleague of mine recently posed the question more tactfully, but his query was essentially this: if the budo are supposed to be all about spiritual enlightenment and the polishing of virtue and all that good stuff, then how come so many budo teachers are such self-indulgent jerks?

Let's make a distinction: we are not speaking here of those teachers of the martial Ways (or at least those who are claiming to be teachers of the martial Ways) who knowingly exploit their students sexually, financially, or in other ways. They are simply frauds and criminals. We are talking here specifically of those sensei who truly, honestly *believe* that they are in the business of promoting spiritual and moral and social values through their instruction at the dojo, when in fact what they are promoting more than anything else is their own ego. The comments of an aikidoka friend present a perfect example.

"I was asked to give a lecture on this very subject at an international aikido training camp," he recalled, "on sensei who behave selfishly and who put their own desires above the needs of their students. Funny thing," he went on, "there were at least four sensei in the audience who were the very sort I was talking about. I was describing them perfectly, I thought, and I was getting a kick as I went on, imagining that I was really making them squirm.

And do you know, three of the four guys came up afterward and congratu-
lated me on spotlighting this problem! They completely missed that I was
talking about them."

The disparity between what some budo teachers say and what they actually do is best understood in light of the thinking of a Chinese philosopher
of the Confucian tradition, Wang Yang Ming, whose ideas had a powerful
influence on the martial Ways of Japan during the latter part of Japan's feudal period. Central to the philosophy evolved by Wang Yang Ming
(1422–1528) is the notion that the individual's highest aspirations in life
should be his efforts to improve himself in order to create a better society.
This may seem like an obvious notion to us today. Yet you must remember
that much of the ethos of feudal Japan was based on ideas that were completely contrary to those of Wang's, ideas that had been formulated by
another Chinese scholar, Chu Hsi (1130–1200). According to Chu Hsi, the
duty of the individual was to perfect himself, the better to serve not society
as a whole but his lord or master. You can probably imagine how enamored
the feudal lords of Japan were with Chu Hsi's philosophy, given that they
needed the absolute loyalty of their samurai if they were to retain their political power. This doctrine could not have served the lords' interests more perfectly. You can imagine, too, how the contrasting principles of Wang Yang
Ming, advocating that one's efforts ultimately ought to be directed inward
for the purposes of creating a better society in general, radically galvanized
the thinking of many of the classical warriors of Japan.

Wang Yang Ming maintained that a person would be making an important step toward self-realization when he pursued the sort of life wherein he
acted on his principles and beliefs. Wang Yang Ming carried this notion one
step further, insisting that to state or to promote a belief and then not to act
accordingly was evidence that one did not really understand that belief in the
first place. Theory and cognitive thought was important to him, but not
nearly as important as the implementation of the ideas expressed through
the intellect. This philosophy is best expressed in the aphorism in Japanese,

toku wa shiru ni yorazu okono ni ari: "Virtue lies not in *knowing* but in *doing.*"

Wang Yang Ming's philosophy sounds a bit anti-intellectual on one level, and in a way it is. Developing ideals and values as part of one's intellect and talking and thinking about them—these are important in the psychological and social growth of the individual. But having these ideals and standards is not as important, according to Wang's view, as acting on them. In a very concrete way, we in the budo are the inheritors of Wang's philosophy of placing the doing above the knowing. In the dojo, "knowing" how to intercept a strike, understanding the kinesiology and physics and principles behind the movement—these are always secondary to the actual physical ability to *do* it.

Wang's thoughts on virtue were not meant to be confined to the arena of training, not for the warrior who followed them sincerely. His philosophy extended to the heart of the spiritual and moral self. The "do as I say and not as I do" school of thought has no tradition or respect in the budo. When you encounter a budo teacher who does not live up to his own professed standards, what you are seeing is a deviation from Wang Yang Ming's philosophy, a philosophy that has guided the thinking of budoka now for many, many generations.

I would venture to guess that Wang's thought particularly appealed to the samurai because it presented a challenging way to live one's life. It is extremely difficult to integrate ideas and deeds, to make the flesh and the spirit, as St. Paul would have put it, come into harmony. Making knowing and doing a simultaneous act is not for the weakling or for those with tendencies to take the easy way out. Indeed, as we can see by the behavior in our politicians and other public figures, not a lot of people in our times are able to espouse—and act on—Wang's philosophy. The dojo, after all, is not the only place where we are apt to find leaders whose words do not match their actions. But you can bet there are few places where the discrepancy is more obvious.

Chapter Forty-five

Moving Toward Stillness

A talent is formed in stillness, a character in the world's torrent.

—Goethe

For budoka there are frustrations. Lots of them. Torments. Distractions. There are setbacks, physical injuries that hold up progress for weeks or sometimes months or longer. And there are the psychological barriers that can be daunting enough to convince us that we won't ever make any more progress. And, of course, there is always the nagging sense of doubt, one often reinforced by others around us who are not engaged in this odd and very foreign quest and who will make it clear that they believe the whole enterprise is rather a silly waste of time. Where exactly is it we are intending to go? they ask us, and we ask ourselves the same question in moments of doubt. Where do we expect the Ways to lead?

Do not kid yourself. Ours is by no means the first generation of budoka to be plagued in this manner. We are linked if by no other connection to those who preceded us, all the way back to the samurai, by the common miseries of our journey. If we are separated from our ancestors in the budo in a significant way, it is not by the doubts and distractions we have all experienced. Rather the difference is that we are not quite sure where we are going on the Way, but our predecessors seem to have had a pretty good idea of their destination as budoka. I cannot claim any special insight into their minds, I hasten to add. Yet when I read the thoughts they left behind, and more vitally for my understanding the budoka of earlier times, when I train in the methods they have passed down, I am struck by a feeling that seems to be expressed time and again. Read their words and you will see the sentiment I am describing.

From the *densho*, the teachings of the feudal era Saburi ryu, a tradition of martial strategy that featured the use of the spear, comes a bit of verse:

> The heart that can hear frost forming in the middle of a cold night,
> when confronted with an opponent,
> will be victorious.

From the written teachings of the Shinkage ryu comes another poem, describing the moment just before swords are crossed and life and death is to be decided:

> A flower, scattering, falls without sound on the moss.
> A flower, scattering, can be heard in the depths of this mountain.

And from dozens of different classical schools of martial strategy we can read of the concept of *suigetsu*, "the moon and the water," advice on keeping the mind as still as the water of a pond, perfectly reflecting the moon.

In each of these writings we find the same message: the search for a deep quiet, a stillness of the soul so profound, so inutterably vast that it is beyond agitation, so intense and concentrated in the core of a human that nothing escapes it, nothing can capture or destroy it.

The budoka who takes this way of being into consideration as the destination for his own martial journey will be brought face to face with a dichotomy. All of the budo involve movement. In most forms of the budo the movement can be quite vigorous. In their execution, the martial Ways are explosive bursts of terrific energy. If it is stillness and quiet you want, then sit in a *zendo*, a hall devoted to the practice of meditation. But the dojo, seems to be the opposite of a place where you would expect to find stillness. As the warrior of old grasped, however, the milieu of the martial Ways was one where motion, the frantic activity of combat, was a route to be traveled to reach this still point.

It is not fair to tell you that such stillness is beyond explaining in words—after all, if it is, then why am I trying to write about it? But I can tell you that the experiences of this stillness are ones that can only be reached through the process of following the Way with both the mind and the body. The budo begin with a training of the gross muscles and then advance to the education and strengthening of the smaller, finer ones and then on to the conditioning of the sinews and ligaments and the reflexes and nerves themselves. Attitudes, feelings, and emotions are all brought into harmony in the process, acting in coordination with the body, and all of this occurs under the aegis of movement and struggle. The movement does not stop, nor does the struggle, not so long as the budoka is alive and able to function at all. But somewhere along this Way, a point of balance is reached. In that balance there is the stillness, the calm in the eye of a great storm. The quiet that hears frost forming on a cold night, that detects the sounds of a flower's petals dropping onto the mossy floor of the valley. A state of being that is as placid as the reflection of the moon on a pond's surface.

It is this stillness toward which we move when we follow a martial Way with sincerity and purpose. It is not an easy trip. The Way is filled with all sorts of difficulties. Don't give up. Stay on the path. Keep moving along the Way. Keep moving toward stillness.

About the Author

Dave Lowry has been involved in the traditional Japanese martial arts and Ways since 1968 and has written about them for more than twenty years. His articles have appeared in magazines in the US, Japan, and the UK. He is the author of seven books on Japan and budo, including *Autumn Lightning* (1985), *Sword and Brush* (1995), and *Persimmon Wind* (Tuttle, 1998). Lowry lives with his wife and child in Missouri, where he is the restaurant critic for *St. Louis* magazine.

ALSO BY DAVE LOWRY AND AVAILABLE FROM
TUTTLE PUBLISHING AND YOUR LOCAL BOOKSTORE:

Persimmon Wind

A Martial Artist's Journey in Japan

Persimmon Wind is a vivid account of the austere journey of a
martial artist, or *bugeisha*—a journey that is, in the end, bittersweet.
The path of the bugeisha is not only a rocky road but a solitary one.
A teacher may set you on the path, but the bugeisha must follow it alone.

ISBN 0-8048-3142-4